CAMBRIDGE LIBRARY COLLECTION

Books of enduring scholarly value

Slavery and Abolition

The books reissued in this series include accounts of historical events and movements by eye-witnesses and contemporaries, as well as landmark studies that assembled significant source materials or developed new historiographical methods. The series includes work in social, political and military history on a wide range of periods and regions, giving modern scholars ready access to influential publications of the past.

The Just Limitation of Slavery in the Laws of God

The author and campaigner Granville Sharp (1735–1813) was born in Durham to a religious family. In 1765, a chance encounter with a slave, Jonathan Strong, sparked the serious interest in abolitionism that in due course saw him become a founding member of the London committee of the Society for the Abolition of the Slave Trade. Due in part to his efforts and writings, the anti-slavery movement in Britain gained public attention and became a more focused and organised campaign. This tract, originally published in 1776, is one of several anti-slavery works that Sharp produced in that year. A rigorous defence of liberty and of 'the honour of holy Scriptures', it is a riposte to the idea that slavery is sanctioned by God, citing the biblical doctrines of 'Thou shalt not oppress a stranger' and 'Love thy neighbour as thyself'. Also included are several appendices of material relating to the abolitionist cause.

The Just Limitation of Slavery in the Laws of God

Compared with the Unbounded Claims of the African Traders and British American Slaveholders

GRANVILLE SHARP

CAMBRIDGE
UNIVERSITY PRESS

CAMBRIDGE UNIVERSITY PRESS

Cambridge, New York, Melbourne, Madrid, Cape Town,
Singapore, São Paolo, Delhi, Mexico City

Published in the United States of America by Cambridge University Press, New York

www.cambridge.org
Information on this title: www.cambridge.org/9781108060158

© in this compilation Cambridge University Press 2013

This edition first published 1776
This digitally printed version 2013

ISBN 978-1-108-06015-8 Paperback

THE
JUST LIMITATION of SLAVERY
IN THE
LAWS of GOD,

COMPARED WITH

The unbounded Claims of the AFRICAN TRADERS and BRITISH AMERICAN SLAVEHOLDERS.

By GRANVILLE SHARP.

With a copious APPENDIX:

CONTAINING,

An Answer to the Rev. Mr. Thompson's Tract in favour of the *African Slave Trade.*—Letters concerning *the lineal Descent of the Negroes* from the Sons of HAM.—The Spanish Regulations for the gradual Enfranchisement of Slaves.—A Proposal on the same Principles for the gradual Enfranchisement of Slaves in *America.*—Reports of Determinations in the several COURTS OF LAW AGAINST SLAVERY, &c.

Take away your Exactions from my People, SAITH THE LORD GOD ! Ezekiel xlv. 9.

LONDON:

Printed for B. WHITE, in Fleet-Street, and E. and C. DILLY, in the Poultry.

M.DCC.LXXVI.

T R A C T I.

THE

Juſt Limitation of Slavery.

THE opinion of the lords Hardwick and Talbot, which I laboured to refute in my Tract againſt *Slavery in England* (1), (printed in 1769,) has ſince been effectually ſet aſide by a clear determination, in the Court of King's-Bench (2), in favour of *James Somerſett, a Negro*, againſt his former Maſter, *C****** S*******, eſq. in the year 1772.

But

(1) A Repreſentation of the Injuſtice and dangerous Tendency of tolerating Slavery in *England*.

(2) See Appendix.

But it is not enough, that the Laws of England exclude *Slavery* merely *from this island*, whilft the grand Enemy of mankind triumphs in a toleration, *throughout our Colonies*, of the moft monftrous *oppreſſion* to which human nature can be fubjected!

And yet this abominable wickedneſs has not wanted advocates, who, in a variety of late publications, have attempted to palliate the guilt, and have even ventured to appeal to Scripture for the fupport of their uncharitable pretenſions: fo that I am laid under a double obligation to anfwer them, becaufe it is not the caufe of *Liberty* alone for which I now contend, but for that which I have ftill much more at heart, the honour of the holy Scriptures, the principles of which are entirely oppofite to the felfifh and uncharitable

uncharitable pretenfions of our **American**
Slaveholders and African Traders.

A late anonymous writer, who calls
himfelf "*An African Merchant,*" remarks, that,—" By the Law of Mofes,
" the Ifraelites might purchafe Slaves
" from the Heathens, and even their
" own people might become Slaves to
" their brethren." *A Treatife on the
Trade from Great-Britain to Africa, &c.
by an African Merchant.* P. 8 *and* 9.

Now, with refpect to the firft part of
his obfervation, it is true, indeed, that
the Ifraelites were expreffly permitted to
keep Bond-Servants, or Slaves, " of the
" *Heathen,* (or, more properly, of the
" *Nations* הגוים) that *were round about*"
them, and of " the children of the ftran-
" gers that fojourned among" them.
(Levit. xxv. 44 to 46.) But we muft remember, that thefe *Heathen,* or " *Na-*

" *tions that were round about them,*" were
an abandoned race of people, already
Slaves and *worſhippers* of devils, and by
them led to debaſe *human nature,* and
to pollute themſelves with the moſt unnatural and abominable vices : " For in
" all theſe," (ſaid the Almighty,) " the
" nations are defiled which I caſt out
" before you : and the Land is defiled ;
" THEREFORE I do viſit the iniquity
" thereof upon it, and the land itſelf vo-
" miteth out her inhabitants,"*&c.* Again;
" For all theſe abominations have
" the men of the land done which
" were before you, and the land is defi-
" led," *&c.* See Levit. xviii. And the
" *children of the ſtrangers,*" abovementioned, were (probably) alſo of the ſame
deteſtable nations of Paleſtine, the Amo-
rites, Canaanites, *&c.* which were ex-
preſſly doomed to deſtruction (3), and
that

(3) " Obſerve thou that which I command thee
" this day : behold, I drive out before thee the Amo-
" rite,

that by the hand of the Ifraelites, *who were commanded to fhew them no pity* (4).

But no doctrine muft be drawn from thefe commands to *execute God's vengeance* upon the faid wicked *ftrangers*, without confidering, at the fame time, *that very contrary treatment of ftrangers* which was *equally* enjoined in the Law : for the Ifraelites were pofitively commanded not to *vex* or *opprefs a Stranger.* " Thou
" fhalt

" rite, and the Canaanite, and the Hittite, and the
" Perizzite, and the Hivite, and the Jebufite. Take
" heed to thyfelf, left thou make a covenant with the
" inhabitants of the land whither thou goeft, left it be
" for a fnare in the midft of thee," &c. Exod. xxxiv.
11 and 12.

(4) " And thou fhalt confume all the people which
" the Lord thy God fhall deliver thee : thine eye fhall
" have *no pity upon them*," &c. Deut. vii. 16. " The
" Lord thy God will put out thofe nations by little and
" little," &c. " The Lord thy God fhall deliver
" them unto thee, and fhall deftroy them with a migh-
" ty deftruction until they be deftroyed. And he fhall
" deliver their kings into thine hand, and thou fhalt
" deftroy their name from under heaven : there fhall
" no man be able to ftand before thee until thou have
" deftroyed them." Deut. vii. 23 and 24.

" *ſhalt love him as thyſelf*," ſaid Moſes,
by the expreſs command of God. " If a
" Stranger ſojourn with thee in your
" land, ye *ſhall not vex*" (or *oppreſs)*
" him. But *the* Stranger that dwelleth
" with you ſhall be unto you as one born
" among you, and *thou ſhalt love him as*
" *thyſelf :* for ye were *Strangers* in the
" land of Egypt." Levit. xix. 33. 34.
And again : " The Lord your God is
" God of gods and Lord of lords, a great
" God, a mighty and a terrible, which
" *regardeth not perſons* nor taketh reward:
" he doth execute the judgement of the
" fatherleſs and widow, and *loveth the*
" *Stranger*, in giving him food and rai-
" ment. *Love ye*, therefore, *the Stran-*
" *ger ;* for ye *were Strangers* in the land
" of Egypt." Deut. x. 17 to 19. In all
theſe paſſages, and many others, the Iſraelites were reminded of their *Bondage
in Egypt :* for ſo the almighty *Deli-
verer* from *Slavery* warned his people
to

to *limit* and moderate the *bondage*, which the Law permitted, by the remembrance of *their own former bondage* in a foreign land, and by a remembrance alfo of his great mercy *in delivering them* from that *bondage* : and he expreffly referred them to *their own feelings*, as they themfelves had experienced the intolerable yoke of Egyptian Tyranny! " Thou fhalt not "*t opprefs a Stranger*; for ye know the " heart of *a ftranger*, feeing ye were " *ftrangers* in the land of Egypt." Exod. xxiii. 9. And again: " Thou fhalt " remember that *thou* waft *a Bond-man* " in the land of Egypt, and the Lord thy " God *redeemed thee*:" Deut. xv. 15.

We muft, therefore, neceffarily conclude, when thefe very oppofite commands are confidered, that the *Heathen*, or *nations* that were " ROUND ABOUT," or in the *environs* of the promifed land, and alfo the *children of the ftrangers*, that

dwelt

dwelt among them, mentioned at the
fame time, whom the Ifraelites were permitted to retain *in perpetual bondage,*
were not intended to be included and
ranked under that general denomination
of *Strangers,* to whom fo much real *af-
fection, benevolence,* and *confideration,* are
ftrictly commanded, in the texts to
which I have juft now referred. And,
confequently, it muft be allowed, that
the particular nations, (the feven nations
of Paleftine, fee Deut. vii. 1.) which
were exprefily devoted to deftruction,
were the only *Strangers* whom the Jews
were permitted to hold in *abfolute Slavery;*
fo that the wicked practice of *enflaving*
the poor *African Negroes* would have
been as *unlawful,* under the Jewifh
Difpenfation, as it certainly is, now
a-days, to Englifhmen, and other fubjects of Great-Britain, that profefs *the
Chriftian Religion; in whofe confideration,*
ALL STRANGERS, from every
other

other part of the world, are, without
doubt, entitled to be ranked, efteemed,
and beloved, *as brethren*, which I have
elfewhere particularly demonftrated; and
which even the law of Mofes expreflly
commanded : — " But *the ftranger*, that
" dwelleth with you, fhall be unto you *as*
" *one born among you*, and THOU
" SHALT LOVE HIM AS THY-
" SELF ; for *ye were ftrangers* in the
" land of Egypt : I am the Lord your
" God." Levit. xix. 33 and 34.

This excellent fyftem of benevolence to
ftrangers, which the Ifraelites were fo
ftrictly enjoined to obferve, cannot, I apprehend, be otherwife reconciled with the
permiffion to the Ifraelites of retaining in
perpetual bondage *the heathen that were
round about them*, and the children of *the
ftrangers* that fojourned among them :
for, if this permiffion were to be extended to *ftrangers in general*, it would

C   fubvert

subvert the exprefs command concerning *brotherly-love* due to *ftrangers*; becaufe a man cannot be faid *to love the ftranger as himfelf* if he holds *the ftranger* and his progeny in a perpetual *involuntary fervitude.* The obfervation therefore of the African Merchant, that " THE ISRAELITES *might " purchafe Slaves from the heathens,"* will by no means juftify the *enflaving* of *modern heathens,* by *Englifhmen,* or by any other nation now fubfifting. The Ifraelites, at that time, might not only purchafe Slaves of thofe particular heathen nations, but they might alfo *drive out thefe heathen*; (I mean, thefe which were particularly named;) nay, even *kill* (5) and *extirpate* them, and *take poffeffion of their cities, houfes,* and *lands.* All thefe acts of violence *might* the Ifraelites do *without fin,* though the like would juftly be efteemed

murder

(5) " But of the cities of thefe people, which the " Lord thy God doth give thee for an inheritance, " thou *fhalt fave alive nothing that breatheth.*" Dout. xx. 16.

murder and *robbery*, if practised by any other nation, not under the like peculiar circumstances : so that the example of the Israelites affords no excuse for the uncharitable practices of the *African Merchant* and *West-India Planter!* The Israelites had an express commission (6) to execute God's vengeance, *without remorse* (7), upon several populous nations, which had rendered themselves *abominable in the sight of*

C 2 *God,*

(6) " Now, therefore, kill every male among the
" little ones, and kill every woman that hath known
" man by lying with him." Numbers xxxi. 17. This
was the judgement against the Midianitish prisoners.
The seven nations of Palestine were likewise subjected
to the same condemnation. " Thou shalt smite them
" and utterly destroy them : thou shalt make no cove-
" nant with them, *nor shew mercy unto them."* Deut.
vii. 2. And a reason for this condemnation was plainly delivered in the fourth verse, to confirm the justice of
it : " For they will turn away thy son from follow-
" ing me, that they may serve other gods."
The Amalekites were also doomed to destruction in
the like manner : " Thou shalt *blot out the remembrance*
" *of Amalek from under heaven* ; *thou shalt not forget it.*
Deut. xxv. 19.

(7) " And thou shalt *consume all the people* which
" the Lord thy God shall deliver thee ; thine eye
" shall have *no pity* upon them. Deut. vii. 16.

God, and therefore deferved no confideration ; fo that *even mercy,* in the Ifraelites,
was a fin (8), when it interfered with this
pofitive command of God !

The commiffion there given, however,
was but *temporary* ; and no other nation,

except

(8) " But, if ye will not drive out the inhabitants cf the
" land from before you, then it fhall come to pafs, that
" thofe, which ye let remain of them, fhall be pricks in
" your eyes and thorns in your fides, and fhall vex you
" in the land wherein ye dwell. Moreover, it fhall
" come to pafs, that *I fhall do unto you* as *I thought to do*
" *unto them.*" Numb. xxxiii. 55 and 56. And the
Ifraelites were exprefsly told, that it was not on their
own account that this extraordinary authority was put
into their hands, but on account of the *abominable wick-*
ednefs of thofe who poffeffed the promifed land.—" The
" land is defiled ; therefore I do vifit *the iniquity there-*
" *of upon it, and the land itfelf vomiteth out her inhabit-*
" *ants.*" Levit. xviii. 25.

" For all thefe abominations" (unnatural lufts,
mentioned in the former part of the fame chapter)
" have the men of the land done which were before
" you ; and the land is defiled." Levit. xviii. 27. And
the Ifraelites were warned againft prefumption, left fuch
extraordinary authority fhould occafion fpiritual pride.
" Not for thy righteoufnefs, or for the uprightnefs of
" thine heart, *aoft thou* go to poffefs the land, but for
" the *wickednefs of thofe nations the Lord God doth drive*
" *them out from before thee,*" *&c.* Deut. ix. 5.

except God's peculiar people, was charged with the execution of it; and therefore, though the Europeans have taken upon themselves, for a long time past, *to attack, destroy, drive out, dispossess, and enslave,* the poor ignorant *Heathen,* in many distant parts of the world, and may, perhaps, plead custom and prescription (to their shame be it said) for their actions, yet, as they cannot, like the Israelites, produce an *authentic written commandment from God* for such proceedings, the offenders can no otherwise be esteemed than as *lawless robbers* and *oppressors,* who have reason to expect *a severe retribution* from God for their tyranny and oppression. It is unreasonable, therefore, to suppose that the severe treatment of the *ancient Heathen,* by the Israelites, under *the dispensation of the Law,* either in *killing, dispossessing,* or *enslaving,* them, should justify our *modern* acts of

violence

violence and *oppreſſion*, now that we profeſs obedience to the *Goſpel of Peace*.

And, with reſpect to the ſecond part of the African Merchant's obſervation, concerning the Iſraelites, *(viz.* that even " their own people might become Slaves " to their brethren,") I muſt remark, that he does not deal fairly by the Jewiſh Law, to quote that circumſtance, without mentioning, at the ſame time, "*the* " *Juſt Limitation*" to which it was ſubject, and the admirable proviſion, in the ſame Law, againſt *the involuntary ſervitude of brethren*; becauſe no Hebrew could be made *a Slave* without *his own conſent*, and even *deſire*, which was to be " *plainly*" and *openly* declared in a court of *record* : — " if the ſervant ſhall *plainly* " *ſay*, I love my maſter, my wife, and " my children, *I will not go out free*, then" (ſays the text) " his maſter ſhall bring " him *unto the Judges*," *&c.* (whereby

an

an acknowledgement *in a court of record* is plainly implied,) " and his master " shall bore his ear through with an aul; " and he shall serve him for ever." Exod. xxi. 5. 6. But, without that *public acknowledgement* of *voluntary consent before the Judges*, the Hebrew master had no authority to bore the servant's ear (9) in token of bondage: and, in every other case, it was *absolutely unlawful* for the Israelite to hold a *Brother Israelite in Slavery!* The Law expressly declares, " If " thy *Brother, (that dwelleth)* by thee, be " waxen poor, and *be sold unto thee; thou* " *shalt not* compel him to serve as a *bond* " *servant: (but)* as an *hired servant*; " and

(9) Yet our inconfiderate West-Indian and American Planters make no scruple even of *branding* their poor Negro-servants with a *hot iron*, to mark them *for perpetual Bondmen, against their will*, though they are certainly their *Brethren* in the eyes of GOD. But GOD hath declared, *expresly*, concerning the crimes of these men, *who enslave the poor*, —— " SURELY, *I will ne-* " *ver forget any of their works! Shall not the land trem-* " *ble for this!*" *&c.! &c.! &c.!* Amos, viii. 7. 8. See also the whole context, from the 4th verse.

" and as a *sojourner* he fhall be with
" thee ; *(and)* fhall ferve thee unto the
" year of jubilee : and *(then)* fhall he
" depart from thee, *(both)* he *and his chil-*
" *dren* with him ;" *&c.* (and the reafon
of this command immediately follows ;)
" for they are *my fervants*," (faid the
Lord,) " which I brought forth out of
" the land of Egypt :" (i. e. *which God*
himfelf delivered from Slavery:) " they
" *fhall not be fold as Bond-men:* thou fhalt
" not rule over him with rigour, but
" *fhalt fear thy God.*" Levit. xxv. 39
to 43. And again, in the 55th verfe,
" For *unto me*" (faid the Lord) " the
" children of *Ifrael are fervants ; they are*
" *my fervants,* whom I brought out of
" the land of Egypt: *I am the Lord*
" *your God.*"

Thus it appears that the *involuntary*
fervitude of *brethren* is entirely inconfiftent with the Jewifh Law ; which, therefore,

fore, is fo far from *juftifying* the *African Merchant*, that it abfolutely *condemns* him. But he is ftill more miftaken, when he infinuates that Slavery is not inconfiftent with the Gofpel. " Jefus Chrift, the " Saviour of mankind and Founder of " our religion," (fays he,) " left the " moral laws and civil rights of mankind " upon their old foundations : his king- " dom was not of this world, nor did he " interfere with national laws : *he did* " *not repeal that of flaves*, nor affert an " univerfal freedom, except from fin : " with him bond and free were accepted, " if they behaved *righteoufly*." *&c.* p. 9.

But how can a man be faid to " behave " *righteoufly*," who fells his *brethren*, or holds them in Slavery *againft their will?* For, though, with Chrift, " *bond* and *free* " are accepted," yet it behoves *the African Merchant* very diligently to examine, whether he is not likely to forfeit his *own*

D   *acceptance,*

acceptance, if he does not moſt heartily repent of having *enſlaved his brethren*, and of having encouraged others to the ſame *uncharitable praĉtices*, by miſinterpreting the holy Scriptures.

Under the Goſpel Diſpenſation, *all mankind* are to be eſteemed *our brethren*. Chriſt commanded his diſciples to go and teach (or make diſciples of) *all nations*, " παντα τα εθνη." Matth. xxviii. 19. So that *men of all nations* (who, indeed, were *brethren* before, by *natural* deſcent from *one common father*) are now, undoubtedly, capable of being doubly related to us, by a *farther* tie of *of brotherhood*, which the law of Moſes ſeemed to deny them, and of which the peculiar people of God (jealous of their own adoption) once thought them incapable; I mean, the ineſtimable privilege of becoming ſons, alſo, to *one almighty Father*, *by adoption*, as well as the Jews, and, conſequently, of being

being *our brethren*, through Chrift, by a
fpiritual, as well as a *natural*, relation-
fhip.

The promifes of God, likewife, in every other part of the New Teftament,
are made to *all mankind in general, without exception*; fo that a Negro, as well as
any other man, is capable of becoming
" *an adopted fon of God*;" an " *heir of God*
" *through Chrift*" (10); a " *temple of the*
" *Holy-Ghoft*" (11); " *an heir* (12) *of*
D 2 " *falva-*

(10)—" that we might receive the *adoption of* Son "
(faid the apoftle, to the Galatians:) " And, becaufe
" *ye are Sons*, God hath fent forth the fpirit of *his Son*
" into your hearts, crying *Abba, Father*: wherefore
" thou art *no more a fervant, but a* Son; and, *if a Son*,
" then an Heir of God through Christ."
Galat. iv. 5. 6. and 7.

(11) " Know ye not that ye are the Temple of
" God, and that the Spirit of God dwelleth in you?
" If any man defile the temple of God, him fhall God
" deftroy; for the *Temple* of God *is holy*, which *Tem-
" ple ye are*." 1 Corinth. iii. 16. 17. See alfo chap.
vi. 19. 20.

(12) " That the Gentiles fhould be *fellow-heirs*,
" and of the fame body, and partakers of his promife
" in Chrift *by the Gofpel*." Ephef. iii. 6.

" *falvation*;" a partaker of *the divine nature* (13); " a *joint-heir with Chrift* (14);
and capable, alfo, of being joined to that
glorious company of Saints, who fhall one
day " *come with him to judge the world*;"
for " the *Saints fhall judge the world.*"
1 Cor. vi. 2. 3. — And, therefore, how
can any man, who calls himfelf a Chriftian, prefume to retain, as a mere chattel,
or *private property*, his fellow man and
brother, who is equally capable with
himfelf of attaining the high dignities
abovementioned! Let Slaveholders be
mindful of the approaching confumma-
tion of all earthly things, when, perhaps,
they will fee thoufands of thofe men,
who were formerly efteemed mere *chattels*

---

(13) —" through the knowledge of him that hath
" called us to *glory* and *virtue* : whereby are given unto
" us exceeding great and precious promifes ; that by
" thefe ye might *be partakers* of the *divine nature.*"
    2 Pet. i. 3 and 4.

(14) " If children, then heirs ; heirs of God and
" joint-heirs with Chrift :" *&c.*   Rom, viii. 17.

tels and *private property*, coming (15) in the clouds (16), with their heavenly Mafter, to judge tyrants and oppreffors, and to call them to account for their want of *brotherly love* !

The Ethiopians, or Negroes, received the Chriftian faith *much fooner* than the Europeans themfelves: their *early* converfion was foretold by the Pfalmift: (Pfalm

(15) — " at the *coming* of our Lord Jesus Christ " *with all his Saints.*" 1 Theff. iii. 13.

— " And Enoch alfo, the feventh from Adam, pro- " phefied of thefe, faying, Behold, the Lord *cometh,* " with *ten thoufands of his faints, to execute judgement upon* " *all,* and to convince all that are ungodly among them, " of all their ungodly deeds," &c. Jude, xiv. 15.

(16) — " and then fhall all the tribes of the earth " mourn, and they fhall fee the Son of man coming in " the clouds of heaven, with power and great glory." Matt. xxiv. 30.

" Behold, he cometh. with clouds, and every eye " fhall fee him : and they alfo *which pierced him :*" Rev. i. 7. And thofe men, alfo, who have worn out their brethren in flavery, may furely be ranked with the wretches that *pierced their Lord.* " — in as much as ye " have done it *unto one of the leaft of thefe my brethren,*" (faid our Lord,) " *ye have done it unto me.*" Matt. xxv. 40. (See the conclufion of my Tract on the Law of Liberty.)

(Pfalm lxviii. 31.) " Princes fhall come
" out of Egypt," (or from *Mizraim)*;
" and Ethiopia" (17) (or *Cufh)* " *fhall*
" *foon ftretch out her hands unto God.*"
And, accordingly, we find the *Ethiopian*
Eunuch (18) particularly mentioned in
Scripture among the firft converts to
Chriftianity:

(17) Wherever we find mention made, in the Old
Teftament, of *Ethiopians*, (though a general name for
Negroes,) yet we fhall find them expreffed, in the
Hebrew, by the name of the eldeft branch of Ham, *viz.*
Chus, כוש. However, we muft remember, that all
Ethiopians are not *Cufhites.* The prodigious army, of a
million of *Ethiopians*, which was overthrown by Afa,
were not all defcendants of *Chus*, though mentioned
under the general name of כושים *Chufim*, in 2 Chron.
chap. xiv. for we read, in the 16th chap. 8th verfe,
that part of that vaft body were *Lubims.* " Were not
" the *Ethiopians* and *Lubims*" (הכושים והלובים)
" a huge hoft?" faid the prophet Hanani, when he
reminded Afa of his former fuccefs. The *Lubims*, or
Libyans, were a great nation, from whom the internal
part of Africa receives its name of *Libya*, and were defcended from Mizraim, the fecond fon of Ham, who
was alfo the father of the Egyptians.

(18) Who might juftly be efteemed *a Prince* of that
country, being Δυναϛης, *a Lord*, or one " *of great autho-*
" *rity* under Candace, Queen of the Ethiopians, *who*
" *had the charge of all her Treafure*," *&c.*

Chriftianity: and that extraordinary exer-
tion of the HOLY SPIRIT, in favour of
the eunuch, was, perhaps, the foundation
of the ancient Church of Habaffi-
nia (19), which, notwithftanding
all worldly difadvantages, remains in
fome degree of *purity* to this day,
as a lafting monument of *Chriftianity
among the fons of Ham*, even in the moft
remote and inacceffible part of Africa!(20)

Certain

(19) The learned Lutholf was of a different opinion,
and fuppofed that the Habaffinians were not converted
till the time of Conftantine the Great, about the year
330; and, though it is not clear whether this latter period was the time of their firft converfion or not, yet,
certain it is, that, ever fince that time, they have
maintained the Chriftian faith, and the facramental in-
ftitutions of Chrift, without yielding to the adultera-
tions of the church of Rome, though the fame were
preffed upon them with all the authority that one of their
own Emperors could exert! Lutholf has given a full
and clear account (printed in 1691) of thefe Chriftian
Negroes and their church, which feems to be referved,
by the providence of God, as a *Witnefs* of the purity
of his holy Religion: a *Witnefs* not lefs remarkable
than the church of the Vaudois!

(20) They ftill retain Water-Baptifm and the holy
Communion *in both kinds*, and drove out the Portuguefe
Jefuits

" Certain it is, (fay the learned Affembly
" of Divines,) that Ethiopia, according
" to this unqueftionable prophecy,"
(Pfalms, lxviii. 31.) " was one of the
" firft kingdoms that was converted to
" the Chriftian faith ; the occafion and
" means whereof we read of Acts viii.
" 27, 28." &c.

The progrefs of the truth muft have
been very rapid in Africa, becaufe we
read of a council of African and Numi-
dian Bifhops, held at Carthage, fo early
as the year of Chrift 215 (21) ; (though
our Anglo-Saxon anceftors remained in
the groffeft pagan darknefs near 400 years
afterwards;) and, in the year 240, a
council of 99 Bifhops was affembled at
Lambefa,

Jefuits for attempting, by force, to pervert and corrupt
thefe *primitive rites*.

(21) " Carthaginenfe 1. circa annum ccxv. fub A-
" grippino, epifcopo Carthaginenfi, ab *Africæ* èt *Nu-*
" *midiæ* epifcopis, *de rebaptizandis hæreticis habitum.*"
Dr. Cave's Hift. Literaria, p. 99.

Lambefa, an *inland city of Africa*, on the confines of Biledulgerid, againft Privatus Bifhop of Lambefa on a charge of Herefie. (22) The fourth Council of Carthage in the year 253 was held by 66 Bifhops, concerning the Baptifm of Infants. (23) And in the eighth Council at that place (anno 256) befides (24) Priefts, Deacons and Laymen, there were prefent 87 Bifhops. In another council of Carthage, about the year 308, no lefs than 270 Bifhops of the Sect of the Donatifts (25) were prefent; and in the year 394, at Baga, an inland City of Africa, 310 (26) Bifhops were collected together, though the

E   fame

(22) Dr. Cave's Hift. Literaria, p. 99.   (23) Ibid.

(24) " Prefentes erant preter Prefbyteros, Diaconos maximamque plebis partem, Epifcopi lxxxvii, &c. See Dr. Cave's Hift. Literaria, p. 100. alfo Bohun's Geog. Dict. p. 219, under the word *Lambefa*.

(25) Dr. Cave's Hift. Lit. p. 222. (26) Ibid. p. 234.

fame was long before the converfion of the Englifh and Dutch, the great traders in *African flaves*; and though the Africans have, fince, lamentably fallen back into grofs ignorance, yet we muft not, on that account, look upon them in the fame light that the Jews did upon "*the children of the ftrangers*," whom they were permitted to hold in flavery (Levit. xxv. 45.) becaufe we cannot do fo without becoming *ftrangers* ourfelves to *Chriftianity*; and haftening *our own apoftacy*, which feems already too near at hand. (27) We may la-
ment

(27) The alarming increafe of infidelity, and the open declarations of Deifts, Arians, Socinians, and others, who deny the Divinity of Chrift, and of the Holy Ghoft, are lamentable proofs of the growing apoftacy! The African Church fell away by degrees in the fame manner, till it was totally loft in the moft barbarous ignorance, (except in Habeffinia) for even thofe Africans who are free from idolatry, and profefs to worfhip *the true God*, are, neverthelefs, enfnared and
enflaved

ment the fallen ſtate of our unhappy
brethren, but we have *no commiſſion
under*

enſlaved in the groſs errors of *Mahometaniſm*, to which
a negl &t of the neceſſary Faith in the *Divinity of Chriſt*,
and of the *Holy Ghoſt*, has an apparent tendency!
We have likewiſe a remarkable inſtance of *infidelity*, or
at leaſt of a total neglect of Scripture authority and re-
velation, in the attempt of two late writers to prove
that Negroes are " *an inferior ſpecies of men :*" but the
learned Dr. *Beattie*, in his *Eſſay on Truth*, has fully
refuted the inſinuations of Mr. *Hume*, the firſt broacher
of that uncharitable doctrine, as well as Ariſtotle's fu-
tile attempt to juſtify *ſlavery* ; ſo that Mr. *Eſtwick's*
ſubſequent attempt, which was prompted only by the
authority of Mr. *Hume*, needs no further confutation.
" That I may not be thought a blind admirer of anti-
" quity, (ſays Dr. Beattie) I would here crave the read-
" er's indulgence for one ſhort digreſſion more, in order
" to put him in mind of an important error in morals,
" inferred from partial and inaccurate experience, by
" no leſs a perſon than Ariſtotle himſelf. He ar-
" gues, ' That men of little genius, and great bodily
" *ſtrength, are by nature deſtined to ſerve*, and thoſe of
" *better capacity to command*; and that the natives of
" Greece, and of ſome other countries, being natu-
" rally ſuperior in genius, have *a natural right to* em-
" pire;

under the Gospel to punish them for it,
as the Israelites had to punish the
Heathens

" pire; and that the rest of mankind, being *naturally*
" *stupid,* are destined to *labour and slavery,*' (De Republ.
" lib. 1. cap. 5, 6) This reasoning is now, alas! of
" little advantage *to Aristotle's countrymen, who have*
" *for many ages been doomed to that slavery,* which, *in*
" *his* judgment, *nature had destined them to impose on*
" *others;* and many nations whom he would have con-
" signed *to everlasting stupidity,* have shown themselves
" *equal* in genius to the most *exalted of human kind.* It
" would have been more worthy of Aristotle, to have
" inferred man's natural and universal right to liberty,
" from that natural and universal passion with which
" men desire it. He wanted, perhaps, to *devise some*
" *excuse for servitude;* a practice which, to *their eternal*
" *reproach,* both Greeks and Romans tolerated even
" in the days of their glory.

" Mr. *Hume* argues nearly in the same manner in
" regard to the superiority of white men over black. ' I
" am apt to suspect,' says he, the negroes, and in
" general all the other species of men, (for there are
" four or five different kinds) to be naturally inferior
" to the whites. There *never was* a civilized nation
" of any other complexion than white, *nor even any in-*
" *dividual* eminent either in action or speculation. *No*
" ingenious

Heathens that were condemned in the
law! Our endeavour fhould be rather
to

" ingenious manufactures among them, *no* arts, *no* fci-
" ences.—There are negro flaves difperfed all over
" Europe, of which *none* ever difcovered any fymptoms
" of ingenuity.' (Hume's Effay on National Charac-
" ters.)—Thefe affertions are ftrong; but I know not
" whether they have any thing elfe to recommend
" them. For, firft, though true, they would *not prove*
" *the point in queftion,* except it were alfo proved, that
" the Africans and Americans, even though arts and
" fciences were introduced among them, would ftill re-
" main unfufceptible of cultivation. The *inhabitants*
" *of Great Britain and France were as favage two thou-*
" *fand years ago,* as thofe *of Africa and America are at*
" *this day.* To civilize a nation, is a work which it
" requires long time to accomplifh. And one may as
" *well fay of an infant, that he can never become a man,*
" *as of a nation now barbarous, that it never can be civi-*
" *lized.* Secondly, of the facts here afferted, *no man*
" *could have fufficient evidence, except from a perfonal ac-*
" *quaintance with all the negroes that now are, or ever*
" *were, on the face of the earth.* Thofe people write
" no hiftories; and all the reports of all the travellers
" that ever vifited them, will not amount to any thing
" like a proof of what is here affirmed. BUT, THIRD-
" LY,

to reftore the *Heathens* to their loft
privileges, than to harden them in
their

" LY, WE KNOW THAT THESE ASSERTIONS ARE NOT
" TRUE. The empires of Peru and Mexico could not
" have been governed, nor the metropolis of the latter
" built after fo fingular a manner, in the middle of a
" lake, *without men eminent both for action and fpecula-*
" *tion.* Every body has heard of the magnificence,
" good government, and ingenuity, of the ancient Pe-
" ruvians. *The Africans and Americans are known to*
" *have many ingenious manufactures and arts among them,*
" *which even Europeans* would find it no eafy matter
" *to imitate.* Sciences indeed they have none, becaufe
" they have no letters ; but in oratory, fome of them,
" particularly the Indians *of the Five Nations,* are faid
" to be greatly our fuperiors. It will be readily allow-
" ed, that the condition of a flave is not favourable to
" genius of any kind ; and yet, *the negro flaves difper-*
" *fed over Europe,* have *often difcovered fymptoms of inge-*
" *nuity, notwithftanding their unhappy circumftances.*
" They *become excellent handicraftfmen, and practical*
" *muficians,* and indeed learn every thing their mafters
" are at pains to teach them, perfidy and debauchery
" not excepted. That a negro flave, who can neither
" read nor write, nor fpeak any European language,
" who is not permitted to do any thing but what his
" mafter

their prejudices by tolerating amongſt
us a greater degree of *deſpotiſm* and *oppreſſion*

" maſter commands, and who has not a ſingle friend
" on earth, but is univerſally conſidered and treated as
" if he were of a ſpecies inferior to the human ;—that
" ſuch a creature ſhould ſo diſtinſtuiſh himſelf among
" Europeans, as to be talked of through the world for
" a man of genius, is ſurely no reaſonable expectation.
" To ſuppoſe him of an inferior ſpecies, becauſe he does
" not thus diſtinguiſh himſelf, is juſt as rational, as to
" ſuppoſe any private European of an inferior ſpecies,
" becauſe he has not raiſed himſelf to the condition of
" royalty.

" Had the Europeans been deſtitute of the arts of
" writing, and working in iron, they might have re-
" mained to this day as barbarous as the natives of
" Africa and America. Nor is the invention of theſe
" arts to be aſcribed to our ſuperior capacity. The ge-
" nius of the inventor is not always to be eſtimated ac-
" cording to the importance of the invention. Gun-
" powder, and the mariner's compaſs, have produced
" wonderful revolutions in human affairs, and yet were
" accidental diſcoveries. Such, probably, were the
" firſt eſſays in writing, and working in iron. Suppoſe
" them the effects of contrivance ; they were at leaſt
" contrived by a few individuals ; and if they required
" a ſu-

preſſion than was *ever permitted among
the Jews,* or even among the ancient
Heathens!

" a fuperiority of underftanding, or of fpecies in the in-
" ventors, thofe inventors, and their defcendents, are
" the only perfons who can lay claim to the honour of
" that fuperiority.

" That every practice and fentiment is barbarous
" which is not according to the ufages of modern Eu-
" rope, feems to be a fundamental maxim with many
" of our critics and philofophers. Their remarks often
" put us in mind of the fable of the man and the lion.
" If negroes and Indians were difpofed to recriminate ;
" if a Lucian or a Voltaire from the coaft of Guinea,
" or from *the Five Nations,* were to pay us a vifit ;
" what a picture of European manners might he prefent
" to his countrymen at his return ! Nor would carica-
" tura, or exaggeration, be neceſſary to render it hi-
" deous. *A plain hiſtorical account of ſome of our moſt
" faſhionable duelliſts, gamblers, and adulterers,* (to name
" no more) would exhibit *ſpecimens of brutiſh barbarity
" and ſottiſh infatuation,* fuch as might vie with any
" that ever appeared in Kamfchatka, California, or the
" land of Hottentots.

" *It is eaſy to ſee with what views ſome modern au-
" thors throw out theſe hints to prove the natural inferiori-
" ty* of negroes. But let every friend to *humanity pray,*
" that

Heathens! for in one of our own *anti-chriſtian* colonies, even the *murder* of a negro ſlave, when under *private* puniſhment, *is tolerated* (ſee the 329th act of Barbadoes) ; and by the ſame diabolical act of aſſembly a man may " of *wantonneſs,* or of *bloody minded-* " *neſs,* or *cruel intention*" (it is expreſsly ſaid) " *wilfully kill* a negro, or *other ſlave* of *his own,*" without any other penalty for it than a trifling fine of

F £15

" *that they may be diſappointed.* Britons are famous for
" generoſity ; a virtue in which it is eaſy for them to
" excel both the Romans and the Greeks. *Let it never*
" *be ſaid, that ſlavery* is countenanced by the braveſt
" and moſt generous people on earth ; by a people who
" are animated with that heroic paſſion, the love of
" liberty, beyond all nations ancient or modern ; and
" the fame of whoſe toilſome, but unwearied, perſe-
" verance, *in vindicating, at the expence of life and*
" *fortune, the ſacred rights of mankind, will ſtrike terror*
" *into the hearts of ſycophants and tyrants,* and excite
" the admiration and gratitude of all good men, to
" the lateſt poſterity." Eſſay on Truth, P. 458, 459,
460, 461, 462, 463 and 464.

£15 fterling. (See remarks on this act
in my tract againft flavery in England,
(28) p. 66 and 67.) Many inftances
of Weft-India cruelty have fallen even
within my own knowledge, and I have
certain proofs of no lefs than three
married women being violently torn
away from their lawful hufbands, (29)
even in London, by the order of their
pretended proprietors! Another remarkable inftance of tyranny, which
came

(28) A reprefentation of the injuftice and dangerous tendency of tolerating flavery in England. London, 1769.

(29) Nothing can be more prefumptuoufly contrary
to the laws of God, than thefe unnatural outrages!
"Have ye not read" (faid Chrift himfelf) "that he
"which made (them) at the beginning, made them
"male and female? and faid, for this caufe fhall a
"man leave father and mother, and fhall cleave to
"his wife: and they twain fhall be one flefh. Wherefore
"they are no more twain, but one flefh. What, there-
"fore, GOD HATH JOINED TOGETHER LET NO MAN
"PUT ASUNDER." Matth. xix. 4, 5 and 6.

came within my own *knowledge*, was
the advertizing a reward (in the Gazetteer
of the 1ft June, 1772) for apprehend-
ing " *an Eaft-India black boy about* 14
" *years of age, named Bob or Pompey :*"
he was further diftinguifhed in the
advertizement by having " *round his*
" *neck a brafs collar*, with a direction
" upon it to a houfe in Charlotte-ftreet,
" Bloomfbury-fquare." Thus the *black
Indian Pompey* was manifeftly treated
with as little ceremony as a *black name-
fake of the dog kind* could be. I inquired
after the author of this unlawful and
fhameful advertizement ; and found,
that he was a merchant even in the
heart of the city of London, who fhall
be namelefs ; for I do not want to
expofe *individuals,* but only their *crimes.*
Now if mafters are capable of fuch
monftrous OPPRESSION, *even here in
England,* where their brutality renders
them

them liable to fevere penalties, how can we reafonably reject the accounts of TYRANNY *in America*, howfoever horrid and inhuman, where the abominable plantation laws will permit a capricious or paffionate mafter, with impunity, to deprive his wretched flave even of life.

I am frequently told, neverthelefs, by interefted perfons from the Weft-Indies, how well the flaves are ufed; and that they are much happier than *our own poor at home.* But though I am willing to believe that *fome few* worthy Weft-Indians treat their flaves with humanity, yet it is, certainly, far from being *the general cafe*; and the mifery of our *own poor* will not be any excufe for *the oppreffion of the poor* elfewhere! When any of our own countrymen *at home* are miferably *poor*, it is not always clear whether themfelves, or others, are to

be

be blamed : all we can know for certain is, that it is the indifpenfable duty of *every man* to *relieve them* according to his ability ; and that the neglecting an opportunity of doing fo, is as great an offence before God as if we had denied affiftance to *Chriſt himſelf* in the fame wretched condition ; for fo it is exprefsly laid down in Scripture, (30) through

(30) " Then ſhall the king fay unto them on his right
" hand,—Come, ye bleſſed of my Father, inherit the
" kingdom prepared for you from the foundation of the
" world ; For I was an hungred, and ye gave me meat :
" I was thirſty, and ye gave me drink : I was a *ſtranger*,
" and ye took me in : naked, and ye clothed me : I was
" ſick, and ye viſited me : I was in priſon, and ye came
" unto me. Then ſhall the righteous anſwer him, faying,
" Lord, when faw we thee an hungred, and fed (*thee*) ?
" or thirſty, and gave (*thee*) drink ? When faw we thee
" a *ſtranger*, and took (*thee*) in, or naked, and clothed
" (*thee*) ? Or when faw we thee ſick, or in prifon, and
" came unto thee ? And the king ſhall anſwer, and
" fay unto them, Verily I fay unto you, inafmuch as ye
" have done (*it*) unto one of the leaſt of theſe my bre-
" thren,

through the mercy of God towards *the
poor :* but it is obvious to whom the
mifery of *a flave* is to be attributed :
for *the guilty poffeffor* will certainly be
anfwerable to God for it ; and every
man, who endeavours to palliate and
fcreen fuch *oppreffion,* is undoubtedly
a partaker of the guilt. The *flaveholder* deceives himfelf if he thinks he
can really *be a* CHRISTIAN, *and yet
hold*

" thren, ye have done (*it*) unto me ! Then fhall he fay
" alfo unto them on the left hand, Depart from me, *ye*
" *curfed into everlafting fire,* prepared for the devil and
" his angels : For I was an hungred, and ye gave me no
" meat ; I was thirfly, and ye gave me no drink : I was
" a *ftranger,* and ye took me not in : naked, and ye
" clothed me not : fick, and in prifon, and ye vifited
" me not. Then fhall they alfo anfwer him, faying,
" Lord, when faw we thee an hungred, or a thirft, or a
" *ftranger,* or naked, or fick, or in prifon, and did not
" minifter unto thee ? Then fhall he anfwer them, fay-
" ing, Verily I fay unto you, *ina much as ye did* (*it*) *not*
" *to one of the leaft of thefe, ye did* (*it*) *not to me.* And
" thefe fhall go away into *ever lafting punifhment :* but the
" righteous into *life eternal."* Matth. xxv. 34—46.

hold such property. Can he be said *to love his neighbour as himself?* (31) Does he behave to others as he would they should to him? " Ye have heard " that it hath been said, *Thou shalt* " *love thy neighbour,* and hate thine " enemy; *but I say unto you* (said our " Lord himself) *love your enemies,* &c. " That ye may be the children of your " Father which is in Heaven : for he " maketh his sun to rise *on the evil,* and " on the good, and sendeth rain *on the* " *juft and on the unjuft;*" (Matth. v. 44, 45) so that *Heathens* are by no mtans excluded from the benevolence *of Chriftians.*

Thus Chrift has enlarged the antient Jewifh doctrine of *loving our neighbours*

as

---

(31) I have examined this point more at large in a tract on " *The Law of Liberty,*" which is intended alfo for publication.

as ourselves; and has alſo taught us, by the parable of the good Samaritan, that *all mankind*, even our *profeſſed enemies* (ſuch as were the Samaritans to the Jews) muſt neceſſarily be eſteemed our *neighbours* whenever they ſtand in need of our charitable aſſiſtance; ſo that the *ſame benevolence* which was due from the *Jew to his brethren of the houſe of Iſrael* is indiſpenſably due, *under the Goſpel*, to OUR BRETHREN OF THE UNIVERSE, howſoever oppoſite in religious or political opinions; for this is the apparent intention of the parable.

No nation therefore whatever, can now be lawfully excluded as *ſtrangers*, according to that uncharitable ſenſe of the word *ſtranger*, in which the Jews were apt to diſtinguiſh all other nations from themſelves; and, ſince *all men* are now to be eſteemed " *brethren and neighbours*"

" *neighbours*" under the Gofpel, none of
the Levitical laws relating to the bondage of *ſtrangers* are in the leaſt applicable to juſtify ſlavery *among Chriſtians*;
though the ſame laws bind *Chriſtians* as
well as *Jews* with reſpect to all the leſ-
ſons of *benevolence* to *ſtrangers*, which
are every where interſperſed therein ; becauſe theſe are *moral doctrines* which
never change, for they perfectly corre-
ſpond with " *the everlaſting Gofpel* "(Rev.
xiv 6.) As for inſtance, " Thou ſhalt *not*
" *oppreſs a Stranger*, for ye know the heart
" of a *Stranger*, ſeeing ye were *ſtrangers*
" in the land of Egypt " Exod. xxiii. 9.
This is an appeal to the *feelings* and experience of the Jews who had themſelves endured a *heavy bondage*, ſo that
it clearly correſponds with the " *royal
law* " or " *law of liberty* " in the Gofpel.

G " *Thou*

" *Thou shalt love thy neighbour as thyself.*"
Gal. v. 14. or as our Lord himself has
more fully expreffed it. " *All things*
" *whatfoever ye would that men fhould*
" *do to you, do ye even fo to them : for*
" THIS IS THE LAW AND THE PRO-
" PHETS. " Matth. vii. 12.

Again, " If a *ftranger* fojourn with thee
" in your land, ye fhall not vex or (opprefs
" him) (*but*) the *ftranger* that dwelleth
" with you, fhall be unto you as one born
" among you, and thou SHALT LOVE
" HIM " (viz. *the ftranger*)" AS THYSELF ;
" for *ye were* STRANGERS in the land of
" Egypt. *I am the Lord your God.*" (Levit.
xix. 33.) Let every flaveholder confider
the importance of this command and
the unchangeable dignity of him who gave
it. " I AM THE LORD YOUR GOD" !--for
the

" the Lord your God is *God* of *Gods,*
" and *Lord* of *Lords,* a *great* God, a *migh-*
" *ty,* and a *terrible,* which regardeth not
" perfons" (not the Mafters more than
any flaves) " nor taketh reward. He doth
" execute the judgment of the fatherlefs
" and widow, and Loveth the stran-
" ger, in giving him food and raiment.
" Love ye *therefore the ftranger* : for ye
" were *ftrangers* in the land of Egypt."
Deut. x. 17, 18, 19. And how can a
man be faid to *love* the *ftranger,* and
much lefs to *love him as himfelf* (fee the
exprefs command above) who prefumes
to vex and opprefs him with a perpetual involuntary bondage? Is this
obedience to that great rule of the Gofpel, which Chrift has given us as the
fum of the law and the prophets? Would
the American flaveholders relifh that con-
temptuous and cruel ufage with which
they opprefs their poor negroes; and
that

that the *African* (31)*ſtrangers* ſhould do
even ſo to themſelves without the leaſt
perſonal provocation or fault on their part,
viz.

(31) The preſent deplorable ſtate of the *African
ſtrangers in general*, ought to warn us of ſimilar judgments againſt the inhabitants of theſe kingdoms ! My
own Grandfather *near a century ago* (wanting only
three years, viz in 1679) warned our great national
counſel of God's vengeance *by this very example,*

" *That* AFRICA (ſays he) which is not now more
" fruitful of monſters, than it was once of excellent-
" ly wiſe and learned men ; that AFRICA which for-
" merly afforded us our Clemens, our Origen, our Ter-
" tullian, our Cyprian, our Auguſtine, and many other
" extraordinary lights in the church of God ; that FA-
" MOUS AFRICA, *in whoſe ſoil Chriſtianity did thrive*
" *ſo prodigiouſly, and could boaſt of ſo many flouriſhing*
" *churches, alas is now a wilderneſs The wild boars*
" *have broken into the vineyard and eaten it up, and it*
" *brings forth nothing but briars and thorns :* to uſe the
" words of the prophet. And *who knows but* GOD *may*
" *ſuddenly make* THIS CHURCH AND NATION, THIS OUR
" ENGLAND, which, Jeſhurun like, is *waxed fat and*
" *grown proud,* and *has kicked againſt God,* SUCH
" ANOTHER EXAMPLE OF THE VENGEANCE OF THIS
" KIND ? "—See arch bp. Sharp's Sermons ſecond vol.
1ſt Serm. which was preached before the houſe of
Commons, April 11. 1679. (Page 22)

viz to be branded with a hot iron, in order to be known and ranked as the cattle and private property of their oppreffors? Like the cattle alfo to be ignominoufly compelled by the whip of a driver to labour hard " *without wages*" or recompence? If the African merchants and American flaveholders can demonftrate that they would not think themfelves injured by fuch treatment from others, they may perhaps be free from the horrid guilt of *unchriftian oppreffion* and *uncharitablenefs*, which muft otherwife inevitably be imputed to them, becaufe their actions will not bear the teft of that excellent rule of the Gofpel abovementioned, which Chrift has laid down as the meafure of our actions—" *All things whatfoever* " *ye would that men fhould do to you, do ye* " *even fo to them, for this is the law and the* " *prophets.*" .Math vii. 12. I muft therefore

fore once more repeat, what I have before advanced, that the permiſſion formerly granted to the Jews of holding
beathens and ſtrangers in ſlavery is vir-
tually repealed, or rather ſuperſeded by
the Goſpel, notwithſtanding the contrary
aſſertion of the African merchant, that
Chriſt " *did not repeal that of ſlaves*"

The *African merchant* has alſo re-
publiſhed the letters of his fellow advocate *Mercator*, who profeſſes in the
ſame manner to draw his authority
"*from Sacred hiſtory*"--" To the ſedate,
" to the reaſonable, to the Chriſtian read-
" ers (ſays he) I ſhall more fully ſet forth
" the *lawfulneſs of the ſlave trade* from the
" expreſs allowance of it in Holy writ :"
(ibid appendix : B. iv.) but the very firſt
inſinuation concerning the origin of ſlave y
which follows this ſpecious addreſs to the
ſedate &c. is founded on two *falſe aſſertions*
even

even in ONE fentence, and therefore I cannot efteem him worthy of any further
notice than that of pointing out thefe
proofs of his little regard to truth ; " As
" to its origin (fays he) it may poffibly be
" derived from that fentence expreffed
" againft Canaan (*from whom the Africans,*
" fays he, *are defcended*) by his father No-
" ah at the hour of his death. (32) Curfed
" be Canaan, a fervant of fervants fhall he be
" to his brethren." But though the author
afterwards allows that " both the origin
" of flavery and the colour of the Africans
" are incapable of *pofitive proof,*" yet the
futility of his infinuation concerning the
defcent

---

(32) It was not " *at the honr of his death,*" but " *when he*
" *awoke from his wine* " after he had tafted too freely the
fruits of the vineyard, which he planted when he began
to be a hufbardman ; the time therefore was probably
very foon after the flood, and not *at the hour of*
death, as mifreprefented by Mercator, for he lived afte
the flood 350 years, Genefis ix. 28.

defcent of the Africans is not like the other two circumftances " incapable of " pofitive proof." For the *Africans* are not *defcended from Canaan,* if we except the Carthaginians (a colony from the fea coaft of *the land of Canaan* who were a free people, and at one time rivalled, even the Roman common wealth, in power. The *Africans* are principally defcended from the three other fons of *Ham,* viz. *Cufh, Mifraim,* and *Phut*; and to prove this more at large I have fubjoined to this tract a letter which I received (in anfwer to mine on the fame fubject) from a learned gentleman who has moft carefully ftudied the antiquities of the line of *Ham* : the infinuation therefore concerning the "*fentence expreffed* " *againft Canaan*" can by no means juftify the *African flave trade,* fo that *Mercator* feems indeed to write like a *mere trader,* for the fake of his iniquitous *Traffic,*

more

more than for the fake of *truth*, notwithftanding his profeffions of regard
for the Holy Scriptures.

If we carefully examine the Scriptures we fhall find, that flavery and oppreffion were ever abominable in the
fight of God; for though the Jews were
permitted by the law of Mofes (on account of the *hardnefs of their hearts*) to
keep flaves, as I have remarked in my
anfwer to the *Reverend Mr. Thompfon*
on this fubject (which is fubjoined,) yet
there was no inherent right of fervice
to be implied from this permiffion, becaufe whenever the flave could efcape
he was efteemed *free*; and it was *abfolutely unlawful* for any man (who be-
lieved the word of God) *to deliver him
up again to his mafter* (fee Deut.
xxiii. 15, 16.) whereas in our colonies, (which in acts of OPPRESSION

H   may

may too juftly be efteemed *antichriftian*)
the flave who *runs away* is " *deemed*
" *rebellious*," and a reward of £ 50 is
offered to thofe who SHALL KILL *or*
" *bring in alive any rebellious flave*" (fee
the 66th act of the laws of Jamaica) By
an act of Virginia (4 Ann, ch 49 § 37
P. 227.) after proclamation is iffued
againft flaves that " *run away and lie*
" *out*" it is " LAWFUL for *any perfon*
" *whatfoever to* KILL and DESTROY
" SUCH SLAVES *by fuch ways and means*
" *as he, fhe, or they* SHALL THINK
" FIT, *without accufation or impeach-*
" *ment of any crime for the fame*," &c.
See the remarks on thefe, and fuch
other *diabolical acts* of plantation affem-
blies in pages 63 to 73, of my reprefentation of the injuftice and dangerous tendency of tolerating flavery in
England. Printed in 1769.

By another act of Virginia, (12
Geo.

Geo. 1. chap. 4, § 8. P 368.) if a poor
fellow is taken up as *a runaway* and
committed to prifon, the goaler may
let him out to hire, in order to pay the
fees, even though he is not claimed,
" *and his mafter or owner* (fays the act)
" *cannot be known* ;" and in a following
claufe the goaler is ordered to " *caufe a*
" *ftrong* IRON COLLAR TO BE PUT ON
" THE NECK *of fuch negroe or runaway*,
" *with the letters* (P. G.) *ftamped thereon* ;"
a moft abominable affront to human nature ! our fpiritual enemy muft have
had a notorious influence with the
plantation law makers to procure an act
fo contradictory to the laws of God, (33)
and

(33) Even white fervants, *Englifh, Scotch, and
Irifh* are frequently taken up by the *fheriff* and *goalers*
without any warrant, or previous judgment whatever, merely " on *fufpicion of being fervants* ;" and
they are then *advertized* to be *delivered up* to their ty-
rannical

and in particular to that (laſt cited)
from Deutrenomy, viz. " Thou ſhalt
" not

rannical maſters ; but though there is great injuſtice
and oppreſſion in taking up theſe poor people merely
" on ſuſpicion *of being ſervants*," yet it does not appear
to be ſo flagrant a breach of God's command beforementioned, as the delivering up the poor runaway *negroes*, who are foreigners, and ſtrangers, and conſequently
leſs capable of obtaining redreſs when they are really
injured : the white ſervants are generally underſtood
to be bound to their maſters only for a ſhort limited
time, either with their own conſent by private contract,
or as felons who are baniſhed their mother country
after a fair trial *by jury* (which excludes any ſuſpicion
of injuſtice) and are ſold for a certain term to pay the
expences of their paſſage, &c. whereby the right of ſervice claimed from them by the maſter is more in the
nature of a *pecuniary debt* than of abſolute ſlavery, ſo
that the white runaway ſervant may perhaps, *as a debtor*,
be delivered up to his maſter without any direct breach
of the law of God beforementioned ; provided there is
no apprehenſion or probability of his being treated with
cruelty on his return ; or that the maſter would be liable to exact more ſervice than is due ; in which caſe
the law ought to afford protection and redreſs ; but no
pretences of this kind can juſtify the *delivering up* a
a negroe *ſtranger !* The poor negroes are claimed *for*
life,

" not deliver unto his mafter the fer-
" vant which is efcaped from his mafter
" unto

life, as an *abfolute property,* though (to compare their
cafe with white fervants) they never offended any
member of our community either at home or abroad to
juftify fuch a fevere punifhment under *Britifh Government ;* neither are they capable of entering into fuch a
legal contract for fervice, as might juftify a mafter's
claim to it, being abfolutely incapacitated by *unlawful
durefs,* to *enter into any contract* as long as they are detained by force or fear in the *Britifh dominions* (for
which *injuftice* to *ftrangers* the *Britifh dominions* muft
fooner or later receive a fevere *retribution*) and therefore *the delivering up to his mafter a negroe fervant*
" THAT HAS ESCAPED FROM HIS MASTER," and has
fince regained his natural liberty, muft neceffarily be
efteemed a fhameful and notorious breach of God's
law. *Neverthelefs our publick prints inform us even of
an Englifh man of war* and another veffel being lately
fent from Grenada to the Spanifh main, " to claim fome
" flaves that had made their efcape from the Iflands,"
(fee Gazetteer June 30, 1773) the writer of the pa-
ragraph alfo expreffes great difappointment on account of the iffue of this unwarrantable and difgraceful
embaffy : " *inftead of meeting with that juftice and*
" *civility which* (favs he) *they had a right to expect, the*
" *Governors at both places, we are told, treated them with*
" *the*

" unto thee ; He fhall dwell with thee,
" among you, in that place which he
" fhall choofe" (that is manifeftly as a
free man) " in one of thy gates *where*
" *it liketh him beft ; thou fhalt not* opprefs
" him". Deut. xxiii. 15, 16. This is
clearly a *moral law,* which muft be ever
binding as the will of *God;* becaufe the
benevolent *intention* of it is *apparent,*
and muft ever remain the fame : for
which

" *the greateft haughtinefs and contempt and refufed to give*
" *them the fmalleft fatisfaction* :" but alas the *very expectation* of better treatment (upon an errand fo unlawful in itfelf, and fo difgraceful to his Majefty's naval
fervice) is a proof of the moft deplorable degeneracy
and ignorance ! Even the cruel Spaniards are more
civilized and fhew more mercy to their flaves at prefent
than the Engiifh, of which their new regulations for
the abolifhing of flavery afford ample proof, though the
RETRIBUTION for their former Tyranny has lately fallen heavily on them according to the laft accounts from
Chiloe and *Chili,* which ought to be confidered as merciful warnings to the reft of the world againft tyranny
and flavery !

which reafon I conclude that AN AC-
TION of TROVER *cannot lye for a flave* ;
and that no man can lawfully be profe-
cuted for protecting a negroe, or any
other flave whatever, that has " *efcaped*
" *from his mafter*" becaufe that would
be punifhing a man for doing *his in-*
difpenfable duty according *to the laws of*
God : and if any law, cuftom or prece-
dent fhould be alledged to the contrary
it muft neceffarily be rejected as *null and*
void; becaufe it is a maxim of the common law of England, that " *the inferior*
" *law muft give place to the fuperior,*
" *man's laws to God's laws*". (attorney
general Noy's maxims P. 19) And the
learned author of the *Doctor* and *Stu-*
dent afferts, that even *Statute law* ought
to be accounted *null and void*, if *it is fet*
forth contrary to the laws of God:
" ETIAM SI ALIQUOD STATUTUM
" ESSE EDITUM, CONTRA EOS NUL-
" LIUS

" LIUS VIGORIS *in legibus Angliæ cenſe-*
" *ri debet, &c*"--- chap, vi.

The degree of ſervitude, which the
Iſraelites were permitted to exact of
their brethren, was mild and equitable,
when compared with the ſervitude
which (to our confuſion be it ſaid) is
common among Chriſtians ? I have already quoted from Leviticus a ſpecimen
of the limitation to the ſervitude of
BRETHREN ; but the Jews were not
only reſtrained *from oppreſſing their*
BRETHREN, but were alſo bound by the
law *to aſſiſt them generouſly and bounti-*
fully according to every man's ability,
when they diſmiſſed them from their
ſervice ; which is a duty too ſeldom
practiced among Chriſtians ! (ſee Deutrenomy xv. 12.) " *If thy brother an*
" *Hebrew man, or an Hebrew woman, be*
" *ſold unto thee, and ſerve thee ſix years ;*
" *then*

" *then in the* SEVENTH YEAR *thou*
" *shalt let him* GO FREE *from thee.* (34)
" *And when thou sendest him* out FREE
" *from thee, thou shalt* NOT LET HIM GO
" AWAY EMPTY : *Thou shalt furnish him*
" LIBERALLY *out of thy flock, and out of*
" *thy floor, and out of thy wine press* :
" (of that) *wherewith the Lord thy God*
" *hath blessed thee, thou shalt give unto him.*
" *And thou shalt remember that* THOU
" WAST A BONDMAN *in the land of* E-
" *gypt,* AND THE LORD THY GOD RE-
" DEEMED THEE : THEREFORE *I* com-
" *mand thee this thing to day.*" These are
the very utmost *limits of servitude* that
we might venture to exact of our brethren *even if we were Jews !* and how much
more are we bound to observe every thing
that is merciful in the law whilst we pro-
fess *Christianity?* What then must we think
of ourselves if we compare these Jewish
I   limitations

(34) See also Exodus xxi. 2.

limitations with our Plantation laws!
A bountiful recompence for the fervice is
plainly enjoined, whereas the whole fubftance perhaps, of the moft wealthy
Englifh or *Scotch* flaveholders would not
fuffice to pay *what is due, in ftrict juftice,*
to thofe who have *laboured in his fervice,*
if the reward is to be proportioned to
their fufferings : but it fhall one day be
required of them --" *Your gold and filver*
" *is cankered; and the ruft of them fhall be*
" *a witnefs againft you, and fhall* EAT
" YOUR FLESH AS IT WERE FIRE : *Ye*
" *have heaped treafure together for the*
" *laft days.* BEHOLD THE HIRE OF
" THE LABOURERS *which have rea-*
" *ped down your fields, which is of you*
" *kept back by fraud,* CRIETH : *and* THE
" CRIES *of them* WHICH HAVE REAPED
" *are eutered into the ears of the Lord*
" *of Sabaoth*" (*or of* ARMIES) James. v.
3 and 4.

The

The *flaveholder* perhaps will fay, that this text is not applicable to him, fince he cannot be faid to have " *kept back by* " *fraud*" *the hire of his labourers*, becaufe he never made any agreement with them for *wages*, having bought their *bodies* of the *flave dealer*, and thereby made them his *own private property*; fo that he has *a right* (he will fay) *to all their labour without wages*. But this is a vain ex-cufe for his *oppreffion*, becaufe it is not fo much *the previous agreement* as the LA-BOUR which renders *wages due* : for " THE LABOURER *is worthy of* HIS " HIRE"(Luke x. 7.) and the fin which " CRIETH *in the ears of the Lord of Sa-*" *baoth*"is the *ufing* a poor man's LABOUR "WITHOUT WAGES;" fo that whether there is an *agreement for wages*, or *no a-greement*, yet, if THE LABOUR *is perfor-med*, the *wages are due*; and thofe, who keep them back, may be faid to *build their houfe in unrighteoufnefs*: as the prophet Jeremiah

Jeremiah has declared in the ſtrongeſt
terms (Jer. xxii. 13.) " *Wo unto him*
" *that buildeth his houſe by unrighteouſ-*
" *neſs, and his chambers by wrong;* (*that*)
" USETH HIS NEIGHBOUR'S SERVICE
" WITHOUT WAGES, AND GIVETH
" HIM NOT FOR HIS WORK."

And the holy Job, even before the
law, declared his deteſtation of UNRE-
WARDED SERVICE. " *If my land* (ſaid he)
" *cry againſt me, or that the furrows like-*
" *wiſe thereof complain:* IF I HAVE EAT-
" EN THE FRUITS THEREOF WITHOUT
" MONEY, *or have cauſed the owners there-*
" *of to loſe there life:* (35) *let thiſtles*
" *grow*

(35) Which was too much the caſe in the late
Engliſh acquiſition of " *the fine cream part of the Iſland*"
of St. Vincent's.—See authentic papers relative to the
expedition againſt the Charibbs. Page 24.

" *grow inftead of wheat; and cockle in-*
" *ftead of barley!* Job. xxxi. 38.---40

The wife fon of Sirach has alfo added his teftimony to the fame doctrine
" *He that defraudeth the* LABOURER *of*
" *his hire is a bloodfheder.* Ecclefiafticus
xxxiv. 22. The flaveholder will perhaps endeavour to evade thefe texts alfo,
by alledging, that though, indeed, he
" *ufeth his neighbour's fervice* WITHOUT
" WAGES, yet he cannot be faid to
" *give him nothing for his work,"* becaufe
he is at the expence of providing him
with food and cloathing (36) and therefore this fevere text is not applicable to
him. But let fuch a one remember (if
he calls himfelf a *Chriftian*) that *Chris-*
tian mafters are abfolutely bound to have
fome regard to *the intereft* of their fervants, as well as to their own *intereft*.
" *Mafters*

(36) Ofnabrug trowfers, and fometimes alfo a Cap

" *Mafters, give unto your* SERVANTS
" *that which is* JUST AND EQUAL, *know-*
" *ing that* YE ALSO *have a* MASTER *in*
" *heaven.*" Collofs. iv. 1.

But *flaveholders* in general, have no
idea of what is " JUST AND EQUAL"
to be given *to fervants* according to the
Scriptures!

It is not a mere fupport in food and
neceffaries, as a mafter feeds his horfe or
his afs to enable the creature to perform
his labour: but as *man* is fuperior to *brutes,*
a further reward is " *juft and equal*" to
be given to the human *fervant.* I have
already fufficiently proved that *every man*
under the Gofpel is to be confidered as
our *neighbour* AND *brother,* and confequently, whatever was " *juft and equal*"
" to be given by a Jew, to his neighbour,
or *Hebrew brother* under the Old Teftament,

ment, the fame muſt, neceſſarily, be conſidered as "*juſt and equal*," and *abſolutely due* from *Chriſtians* to men of *all nations* without diſtinction, whom we are bound to treat *as brethren* under the Goſpel *in whatever capacity they ſerve us.* Let the American *ſlaveholder* therefore remember, that *even according to the Jewiſh law,* (if he argues upon it *as a* CHRISTIAN *ought to do*) he is abſolutely indebted to each of his ſlaves *for every days labour* BEYOND *the firſt ſix years* OF HIS SERVITUDE. " *In the* SEVENTH " *year* (ſaid the Lord by Moſes,) *thou* "*ſhalt let him* GO FREE *from thee. And* " *when thou ſendeſt him out* FREE *from thee,* " *thou* SHALT NOT LET HIM GO AWAY " EMPTY . *Thou ſhalt furniſh him* LI-" BERALLY *out of thy* FLOCK, &c. " *wherewith the Lord thy God hath bleſs-* " *ed thee, thou ſhalt give unto him*" &c.

If

If this was the indifpenfable duty *even of Jews!* how much more is it " JUST AND EQUAL to be obferved by *Chriftians ?* The fame command, when applied to the *American planter*, will include a proper ftock of plants for cultivation, as Sugar-Canes, Tobacco, Indigo, &c. as well as cattle and ftores, to enable a poor man to maintain himfelf and family upon a fmall farm, or lot of fpare ground, lett, for a certain limitee time, on reafonable terms; and renewable on equitable conditions; which are the only true means of reducing *the price of labour*, and *provifions.* Let not the planter *grudge* to part with his *fervant* when he has *ferved* a reafonable time in proportion to *his price*, (agreeable for, inftance, to the regulations adopted by the *Spaniards* which I have already recommended to the *Englifh* planters See Appendix 5.) for the word of God forbids any fuch bafe reluctance. " *It fhall not* " SEEM
" HARD

" SEEM HARD UNTO THEE *when thou*
" *fendeſt* HIM AWAY FREE *from thee; for*
" *he hath been worth a double hired ſer-*
" *vant* (to thee) *in ſerving thee ſix years* :
" *and the* Lord *thy God ſhall bleſs thee in*
" *all that thou doeſt."* Deut. xv. 18

The ſlaveholder perhaps will alledge
that, though the Jews were bound to
ſhew this benevolence to their *brethren*
of Iſrael, yet the ſame laws do not bind
the American planter, becauſe his ſlaves
are for the moſt part *heathens* or (as ſome
of the negroes are) *Mahometans*, and
therefore he is not bound to conſider
them as his *brethren* ; being rather juſtified by the law, which permitted the
Jews to keep *heathen ſlaves*, and " *the*
" *children of the ſtrangers,"* in perpetual
bondage &c They ſhall be your *bondmen*
for ever--ſee Leviticus xxv. 44, 45, and
46 --But I have already guarded againſt

K   this

this objection, in the former part of this
tract; and it muft clearly appear, by
the feveral points fince mentioned, that
as Chriftians, we muft not prefume to
look upon any man whatever in the
fame light that the *Ifraelites* once did
upon " *the children of the ftrangers,*"
whether they be *black* or *white, Heathens* or *Mahometans.*

If a *Heathen,* or a *Mahometan,* happens
to fall into our hands, fhall we confirm
his prejudices by *oppreffion,* inftead of
endeavouring to inftruct him as a *brother?* Surely the blood of fuch a poor
infidel muft reft on the guilty head of
that *nominal* Chriftian, who neglects
the opportunity of adding to the number of *his brethren* in the Faith! And
therefore, let that man, who endeavours
to deprive others of their juft privileges
as *brethren,* take heed left he fhould thereby unhappily occafion his *own rejection*
in

in the end, when that dreadful doom,
which the uncharitable muſt expect
will certainly be pronounced!—For
then " *the* KING" (the King of King's)
" *ſhall anſwer, and ſay unto them,—*
" *Verily I ſay unto you,—In as much as*
" *ye have done* (it) *unto one* of *the leaſt*
" *of theſe* MY BRETHREN," (for that
glorious KING will eſteem even the
meaneſt SLAVES as HIS BRETHREN, if
they believe in him,) "*ye have done* (it)
" *unto* ME ! DEPART FROM ME YE
" CURS D *into everlaſting Fire, pre-*
" *pared for the Devil and his Angels.*"
" (Matt. xxv. 40, 41.) *I know you not !*
" (xxv. 12.)—*I never knew you ;—De-*
" *part from me ye that work iniquity !*"
(Matt. vii. 23.)

Soli Deo Gloria et Gratia.

F I N I S

APPENDIX

(N°. 1.)

========================

An ESSAY on

SLAVERY,

Proving from SCRIPTURE its Inconsiftency
with HUMANITY and RELIGION;

By GRANVILLE SHARP.

" With an introductory PREFACE," (*by a Gentleman
of the Law, in Weft Jerfey*) " containing the Sen-
timents of the Monthly Reviewers on a Tract,
by the Rev. T. Thompfon, *in Favour* of the *Slave
Trade*."

---

*The Lord alfo will be a Refuge for the Oppreffed—
a Refuge in Time of Trouble,* Pfalm. ix- 9.

========================

BURLINGTON: WEST JERSEY,
Printed, M.DCC.LXXIII.

LONDON: reprinted, 1776.

Preface by the American Editor.

' THE following Effay, though wrote,
' as the Author fignifies, in hafte,
' is thought to have fuch merit as
' to deferve a publication.—The copy was
' fent to one of the Writer's particular
' friends, whether for his own peculiar fa-
' tisfaction, or the prefs, is uncertain ; but
' as the fubject is *Liberty*, fo it is expected
' the *Freedom* which is here taken, cannot
' juftly give him offence, or be unaccepta-
' ble to the public.'

' It was defigned to confute a piece wrote
' by Thomas Thompfon, M. A. fome time
' fellow of C. C. C. entitled,' " The Afri-
" can trade for Negro Slaves fhewn to be
" confiftent with principles of humanity,
" and with the laws of revealed religion."
' Printed at Canterbury.'

' In order to fhew that the Effay Writer
' has not mifreprefented the text, nor is
' fingle in his obfervations upon it, the fen-
' timents of the Monthly Reviewers on that
' pamphlet in May, 1772, are here infert-
' ed.'

" We muft acknowledge," fay they, " that
" the branch of trade here under confidera-

" tion, is a fpecies of traffic which we have
" never been able to reconcile with the dic-
" tates of humanity, and much lefs with
" thofe of religion. The principal argu-
" ment in its behalf feems to be, the *necef-*
" *fity* of fuch a refcource, in order to carry
" on the works in our plantations, which,
" we are told, it is otherwife impoffible to
" perform. But this, though the urgency
" of the cafe may be very great, is not by
" any means fufficient to juftify the prac-
" tice. There is a farther confideration
" which has a plaufible appearance, and
" may be thought to carry fome weight ;
" it is, that the merchant only purchafes
" thofe who were flaves before, and poffi-
" bly may, rather than otherwife, render
" their fituation more tolerable. But it is
" well known, that the lot of our Slaves,
" when moft favourably confidered, is very
" hard and miferable ; befides which, fuch
" a trade is taking the advantage of the ig-
" norance and brutality of unenlightened na-
" tions, who are encouraged to war with
" each other for this very purpofe, and, it
" is to be feared, are fometimes tempted to
" feize thofe of their own tribes or families
" that they may obtain the hoped for ad-
" vantage : and it is owned, with regard to
" our merchants, that, upon occafion, they
" obferve the like practices, which are
                              " thought

" thought to be allowable, becaufe they
" are done by way of reprifal for theft
" or damage committed by the natives. We
" were pleafed, however, to meet with a
" pamphlet on the other fide of the quef-
" tion ; and we entered upon its perufal
" with the hopes of finding fomewhat ad-
" vanced which might afford us fatisfaction
" on this difficult point. The writer ap-
" pears to be a fenfible man, and capable
" of difcuffing the argument ; but the li-
" mits to which he is confined, rendered
" his performance rather fuperficial. The
" plea he produces from the Jewifh law is
" not, in our view of the matter, at all
" conclufive. The people of Ifrael were
" under a *theocracy*, in which the Supreme
" Being was in a peculiar fenfe their King,
" and might therefore iffue forth fome or-
" ders for them, which it would not be
" warrantable for another people, who were
" in different circumftances, to obferve.
" Such, for inftance, was the command
" given concerning the extirpation of the
" Canaanites, whom, the fovereign Arbiter
" of life and death might, if he had pleafed,
" have deftroyed by plague or famine, or
" other of thofe means which we term na-
" tural caufes, and by which a wife Provi-
" dence fulfils its own purpofes. But it
" would be unreafonable to infer from the
                                        manner

" manner in which the Ifraelites dealt with
" the people of Canaan, that any other na-
" tions have a right to purfue the fame me-
" thod.   Neither can we imagine that St.
" Paul's exhortation to fervants or flaves,
" upon their converfion, to continue in the
" ftate in which chriftianity found them,
" affords any argument favourable to the
" practice here pleaded for.   It is no more
" than faying, that Chriftianity did not
" particularly enter into the regulations of
" civil fociety at that time ; that it taught
" perfons to be contented and diligent in
" their ftations : but certainly it did not
" forbid them, in a proper and lawful way,
" if it was in their power, to render their
" circumftances more comfortable.   Upon
" the whole, we muft own, that this little
" treatife is not convincing to us, though, as
" different perfons are differently affected
" by the fame confiderations, it may prove
" more fatisfactory to others."
    ' In another place they obferve,' " fince
" we are *all brethren*, and God has given to
" *all* men a natural right to *Liberty*, we al-
" low of no *Slavery* among us, unlefs a per-
" fon forfeits his freedom by his crimes "
    ' That Slavery is not confiftent with the
' Englifh conftitution, nor admiffable in
' Great Britain, appears evidently by the
' late folemn determination, in the court of
                                        ' King's

King's Bench at Weſtminſter, in the caſe
‘ of James Somerſet, the Negro ; and why
‘ it ſhould be revived and continued in the
‘ colonies, peopled by the deſcendents of
‘ Britain, and bleſſed with ſentiments as
‘ truly noble and free as any of their fellow
‘ ſubjects in the mother country, is not eaſi-
‘ ly conceived, nor can the diſtinction be
‘ well founded.’

 ‘ IF “ natural rights, ſuch as *life* and *Li-*
“ *berty*, receive no additional ſtrength from
“ municipal laws, nor any *human legiſlature*
“ has *power* to abridge or *deſtroy them*, un-
“ leſs the owner commits ſome act that a-
“ mounts to a forfeiture;” *(a)* ‘ If “ the
“ natural *Liberty of mankind* conſiſts proper-
“ ly in a power of acting as one thinks fit,
“ without any reſtraint or controul unleſs
“ by the *law of nature* ; being a *right inhe-*
“ *rent in us by birth*, and one of the *Gifts of*
“ *God to man* at his creation, when he en-
“ dued him with the faculty of *free will* :”
(b) ‘ If an *act of Parliament* is *controulable*
‘ *by the laws of God and nature* ; *(c)* and *in*
‘ *its conſequences* may be *rendered void for*
‘ abſurdity, or a *manifeſt contradiction to*
‘ *common reaſon* : *(d)* If “ Chriſtianity is a
“ part of the law of England ;” *(e)* and
　　　　　　　　　　　　　　“ Chriſt

(a). 1 Blackſtone's Commentaries, 54.　*(b)* Dit.
125. *(c)* 4 Bacon's Abridg. 639.　*(d)* 1 Black.
Com. 91. *(e)* Stra. Reports, 1113.

' Chrift exprefsly commands, " Whatfoever
" ye would that men fhould do to you, do
" ye even fo to them;" ' at the fame time
' declaring,' " for this is the law and the
" law and the prophets," (f) ' And if
' our forefathers, who emigrated from Eng-
' land hither, brought with them all the
' rights, liberties, and privileges of the
' Britifh conftitution—(which hath of late
' years been often afferted and repeatedly
' contended for by Americans) why is it
' that the poor footy African meets with fo
' different a meafure of juftice in England
' and America, as to be *adjudged free* in
' the one, and in the other held in the moft
' *abjeɛ̄ Slavery?*

' WE are exprefsly reftrained from mak-
' ing laws, " repugnant to," and directed
' to fafhion them, " as nearly as may be,
" agreeable to, the laws of England."
' Hence, and becaufe of its total inconfif-
' tency with the principles of the conftitu-
' tion, neither in England or any of the
' Colonies, is there one law directly in fa-
' vour of, or enaɛ̄ing *Slavery*, but by a
' kind of fide wind, admitting its exiftence,
' (though only founded on a barbarous
' cuftom, originated by foreigners) attempt
' its regulation. How far the point liti-
' gated in James Somerfet's cafe, would
                                    ' bear

(a) Matt. vii. 12.

' bear a fober candid difcuffion before an
' impartial judicature in the Colonies, I
' cannot determine; but, for the credit of
' my country, fhould hope it would meet
' with a like decifion, that it might appear
' and be known, that *Liberty* in America,
' is not a partial privilege, but extends to
' every individual in it.'

　' I MIGHT here, in the language of the
' famous JAMES OTIS, Efq; afk, " Is it
" poffible for a man to have a natural right
" to make a Slave of himfelf or his pofteri-
" ty ? What man is or ever was born free,
" if every man is not ? Can a father fuper-
" fede the laws of nature ? Is not every man
" born as f ee by nature as his father ? (*a*)
" There can be no prefcription old enough
" to fuperfede the law of nature, and the
" grant of God Almighty, who has given
" to every man a natural right to be free.
" (*b*)　The Colonifts are by the law of na-
" ture free born, as indeed all men are,
" white or black.　No better reffon can be
" given for the enflaving thofe of any co-
" lour, than fuch as Baron Montefquieu has
" humouroufly affigned, as the foundation
" of that cruel Slavery exercifed over the
" poor Ethiopeans; which threatens one
" day to reduce both Europe and America
　　　　　　　b　　　　　　　　　" to

(*a*) 1 American Tracts by Otis, 4.　　(*b*) American Tracts by Otis, 17.

" to the ignorance and barbarity of the
" darkeſt ages. Does it follow that it is
" right to enſlave a man bec uſe he is black ?
" Will ſhort curled hair like wool, inſtead
" of chriſtians hair, as it is called by thoſe
" whoſe hearts are hard as the nether mill-
" ſtone, help the argument ? Can any lo-
" gical inference in favour of Slavery, be
" drawn from a flat noſe‖ a long or a ſhort
" face ? Nothing better can be ſaid in fa-
" vour of *a trade* that is the moſt ſhocking
" violation of the laws of nature ; has a
" direct tendency to diminiſh every idea of
" the ineſtimable value of Liberty, and
" makes every dealer in it a tyrant, from
" the director of an African company, to
" the petty chapman in needles and pins,
" on the unhappy coaſt." (*a*)

‘ To Thoſe who think Slavery founded in
‘ Scripture, a careful and attentive peruſal
‘ of the Sacred Writings would contribute
‘ more than any thing to eradicate the er-
‘ ror, they will not find even the name of
‘ *Slave* once mentioned therein, and applied
‘ to a ſervitude to be continued from parent
‘ to child in perpetuity, with approbation.
‘ —The term uſed on the occaſion in the
‘ ſacred text is *Servant* ; and, upon a fair
‘ conſtruction of thoſe writings, there is no
‘ neceſſity, nor can the ſervice, conſiſtent
                                        ‘ with

(*a*) American Tracts, 43, 44.

‘ with the whole tenor of the Scripture, be
‘ extended further than the generation fpo-
‘ ken of ; it was never intended to include
‘ the pofterity.

‘ THE miftaken proverb which prevailed
‘ in that early age, " The fathers had ea-
" ten four grapes, and the childrens teeth
" were fet on edge," was rectified by the
prophets Jeremiah and Ezekiel, who declared to the people, that " they fhould not
" have occafion to ufe that proverb any
" more ;—Behold all fouls are mine, as the
" foul of the father, fo the foul of the fon,
" the foul that finneth it fhall die ;—the fon
" fhall not bear the iniquity of the father,
" neither fhall the father bear the iniquity
" of the fon ;—the righteoufnefs of the
" righteous fhall be upon him, and the
" wickednefs of the wicked fhall be upon
" him. (a) ‘ And the apoftle Peter affures
‘ us, after the afcenfion of our Saviour, that
" God is no refpecter of perfons, but in
" every nation he that feareth him is ac-
" cepted of him." (b) ‘ It is alfo remark-
‘ able, that at that time, an Ethiopian, " a
" man of great authority," (c) was ad-
‘ mitted to the freedom of a Chriftian,
‘ whatever we may think of the colour now,
‘ as being unworthy of it.

b 2   ‘ But

(a) Jer. xxxi. 29.   Ezek. xviii. 3, 4, and 20,
(b) Acts x. 34.   (c) Ditto, viii. 27.

' But admitting Slavery to be eftablifhed
' by Scripture, the command of the Sove-
' reign Ruler of the univerfe, whofe eye'
' takes in all things, and who, for good
' reafons, beyond our comprehenfion, might
' juftly create a perpetual Slavery to effect
' his own purpofes, againft the enemies of
' his chofen people in that day, cannot be
' pleaded now againft any people on earth ;
' it is not even pretended to in juftification
' of Negro Slavery, nor can the fons of.
' Ethiopia, with any degree of clearnefs, be
' proved to have defcended from any of
' thofe nations who fo came under the Di-
' vine difpleafure as to be brought into fer-
' vitude; if they are, and thofe denuncia-
' tions given in the Old Teftament were
' perpetual, and continue in force, muft we
' not look upon it meritorious to execute
' them fully upon all the offspring of that
' unhappy people upon whom they fell,
' without giving quarter to any ?'

' MANY who admit the indefenfibility
' of Slavery, confidering the fubject rather
' too fuperficially, declare it would be im-
' politic to emancipate thofe we are poffeffed
' of ; and fay, they generally behave ill
' when fet at liberty. I believe very few
' of the advocates for freedom think that
' all ought to be manumitted, nay, think
' it would be unjuft to turn out thofe who
' have

‘ have ſpent their prime of life, and now
‘ require a ſupport ; but many are in a
‘ fit capacity to do for themſelves and the
‘ public ; as to theſe let every maſter or
‘ miſtreſs do their duty, and leave conſe-
‘ quences to the Diſpoſer of events, who,
‘ I believe, will always bleſs our actions in
‘ proportion to the purity of their ſpring.
‘ But many inſtances might be given of
‘ Negroes and Mulatoes, once in Slavery,
‘ who, after they have obtained their li-
‘ berty, (and ſometimes even in a ſtate of
‘ bondage) have given ſtriking proofs of
‘ their integrity, ingenuity, induſtry, ten-
‘ derneſs and nobility of mind ; of which,
‘ if the limits of this little Piece permit-
‘ ed, I could mention many examples ; and
‘ why inſtances of this kind are not more fre-
‘ quent, we may very naturally impute to
‘ the ſmallneſs of the number tried with
‘ freedom, and the ſervility and meanneſs of
‘ their education whilſt in Slavery. Let us
‘ never forget, that an equal if not a grea-
‘ ter proportion of our own colour behave
‘ worſe with all the advantages of birth,
‘ education and circumſtances ; and we
‘ ſhall bluſh to oppoſe an equitable emanci-
‘ pation, by this or the like arguments.

    “ LIBERTY, the moſt manly and exalt-
“ ing of the gifts of Heaven, conſiſts in a
“ free and generous exerciſe of all the hu-
                                    “ man

" man faculties as far as they are compati-
" ble with the good of fociety to which we
" belong ; and the moft delicious part of
" the enjoyment of the ineftimable blefling
" lies in a confcioufnefs that we are *free*.
" This happy perfuafion, when it meets
" with a noble nature, raifes the foul, and
" rectifies the heart ; it gives dignity to the
" countenance and animates every word and
" gefture ; it elevates the mind above the
" little arts of deceit, makes it benevolent,
" open, ingenuous and juft, and adds a new
" relifh to every better fentiment of huma-
" nity." (*a*) On the contrary, " Man is
" bereaved of half his virtues that day when
" he is caft into bondage." (*b*)

' THE end of the chriftian difpenfation,
' with which we are at prefent favoured, ap-
' pears in our Saviours words,' " The fpi-
" rit of the Lord is upon me, becaufe he
" hath anointed me to preach the gofpel to
" the poor ; he hath fent me to heal the *bro-*
" *ken hearted*; to preach deliverance to the
" captives ; and recovery of *fight to the blind*;
" to fet at *liberty them that are bruifed* ; to
" preach the *acceptable year of the Lord*." (*c*)

' THE Editor is united in opinion with the
' author of the Eflay, that flavery is contra-
' ry to the laws of reafon, and the principles
' of

(*a*) Blackwell's Court of Auguflus. (*b*) Homer.
(*c*) Luke iv. 18.

' of revealed religion ; and believes it alike
' inimical and impolitick in every ftate and
' country ; for as " righteoufncfs exalteth a
" nation, fo fin is a reproach to any people."
' (a) Hence whatever violates the purity of
' equal juftice, and the harmony of true li-
' berty, in time debafes the mind, and ulti-
' mately draws down the difpleafure of that
' Almighty Being, who " is of purer eyes
" than to behold evil, and cannot look on ini-
" quity ." (b) ' Yet he is far from cenfuring
' thofe who are not under the fame convic-
' tions, and hopes to be underftood with cha-
' rity and tendernefs to all. Every one does
' not fee alike the fame propofitions, who
' may be equally friends to truth, as our
' education and opportunities of knowledge
' are various as our faces. He will candidly
' confefs to any one who fhall kindly point
' it out: any error which in this inquiry hath
' fell from his pen. There can be but one
' beatific point of rectitude, but many paths
' leading to it, in which perfons differing in
' mode and non effentials, may walk with
' freedom to their own opinions ; we may
' much more innocently be under a miftake,
' than continue in it after a hint given,
' which occafions our adverting thereto ; for
' it feems a duty to inveftigate the way of
' truth

(a) Prov. xiv. 34. (b) Habakuk i, 13.

' truth and juftice with our utmoft ability.

' A much more extenfive and perfect view
' of the fubject under confideration, has of
' late prevailed than formerly ; and he be-
' lieves nothing is wanting but an impartial
' difinterefted attention to make ftill greater
' advances. Thus, by a gradual progreffion,
' he hopes the name of *Slavery* will be eradi-
' cated by the general voice of mankind in
' this land of *Liberty*.

' The mode of manumitting negroes in
' New-Jerfey is fuch as appears terrific, and
' amounts almoft to a prohibition, becaufe of
' its incumbering confequences, which few
' prudent people chufe to leave their fa-
' milies liable to. It is much eafier in fe-
' veral other colonies. In Pennfylvania a
' recognizance entered into in Thirty
' Pounds to indemnify the townfhip, is a
' compleat difcharge In Mariland, where
' Negroes are fo numerous, I am informed,
' the mafter or miftrefs may at pleafure
' give Liberty to their flaves without the
' leaft obligation, and be clear of any future
' burden. Both the e are exceptionable;
' and may be improved. Proper diftinctions
' are neceffary ; for as the freedom of all
' gratis might be unjuft, not only to the
' publick but the Slave : fo any clog upon
' the owner who gives up his right at an
' age when he cannot have received much
' or any advantage from the labour of the
                                    ' individual

' individual, would be unreafonable. The
' wifdom of a legiflature earneftlv difpofed
' to do good, will I hope be directed to fur-
' mount every little difficulty in pointing
' out a fcheme more equal and perfect, by
' fteering a middle courfe ; and proper care
' being kindly taken to affift and provide for
' the ufefulnefs of thofe deferving objects of
' benevolence, the approbation of Divine
' Providence will I doubt not, attend fuch
' laudable endeavours, and crown them with
' fuccefs. — That the legiflative body of each
' province in America may give due atten-
' tion to this important engaging fubject,
' and be bleffed to frame and eftablifh a
' plan worthy of the united jurifprudence,
' wifdom, and benevolence of the *Guardians*
' *of Liberty,* is the fincere wifh of'

THE E D I T O R.

N

A N

ESSAY on SLAVERY,

Proving from Scripture its inconfiften-
cy, with Humanity and Religion,

By GRANVILLE SHARP.

A REVEREND author, Mr. Thomas Thompfon, M. A. has late-
ly attempted to prove " that the Afri-
" can trade for Negroe Slaves is con-
" fiftent with the principles of *humanity*
" and *revealed religion.*"

FROM Leviticus xxv. 39 to 46, he draws
his principle conclufion, viz. " that the
" buying and felling of Slaves *is not con-*
" *'rary to the law of nature*, for (fays
" he)

[19]

" he) the *Jewish conftitutions* were
" ftrictly therewith confiftent *in all*
" *points* : and thefe are in certain cafes
" the rule by which is determined by
" *learned lawyers* and cafuifts, what is,
" or is not, *contrary to nature.*" I have
not leifure to follow this author me-
thodically, but will, neverthelefs, examine his ground *in a general way,* in
order to prevent any ill ufe that may be
made of it againft the important queftion
now depending before the judges. *(a)*

THE reverend Mr. Thompfon's *premifes are not true,* for the Jewifh conftitutions *were not "ftrictly confiftent"*
with the *law of nature* in all points, as
he fuppofes, and confequently his principal *conclufion* thereupon is erroneous.
Many things were formerly tolerated
among the Ifraelites, merely through
the

(*a*) Meaning I fuppofe, (fays the American editor)
the cafe of Somerfet, which then depended.

the mercy and forbearance of God, in confideration of their extreme frailty and inability, at that time, to bear a more perfect fyftem of law. Other laws there are in the five books (befides the ceremonial laws now abrogated) which are merely *municipal,* being adapted to the peculiar polity of the Ifraelitifh commonwealth, on account of its fituation in the midft of the moft barbarous nations, whom the Hebrews were at all times but too much inclined to immitate.

THE univerfal *moral laws* and thofe of *natural equity* are, indeed, every where plentifully interfperfed among the *peculiar laws* abovementioned; but they may very eafily be diftinguifhed by every fincere Chriftian, who examines them with *a liberal mind,* becaufe the *benevolent purpofe* of the Divine Author

is

is *always apparent* in thofe laws which
are to be *eternally binding* ; for " it is
" *the reafon* of the law which confti-
" tutes the *life of the law,*" according to
an allowed maxim of our own country,
" Ratio Legis eft anima Legis," (Jenk.
Cent. 45.) And with refpeſt to thefe
moral and *equitable* laws, I will readily
agree with the Reverend Mr. Thompfon, that they are the beft rule by which
" learned judges and cafuifts can deter-
" mine what is, or is not, *contrary to*
" *nature.*"

BUT I will now give a few examples
of laws, which are in *themfelves contrary to nature or natural equity,* in order
to fhew that Mr. Thompfon's *premifes*
are totally falfe :

THE Ifraelites were exprefsly *permitted
by the law of Mofes* to give a bill of di-
vorce

vorce to their wives whenever they pleafed, and to marry *other women*; and the women who were put away, were alfo exprefsly permitted, by the Mofaic law, *to marry again*, during the lives of their for mer hufbands.

ALL which practices were manifeftly contrary to *the law of nature* in its purity, though not perhaps to *the nature of our corrupt affections and defires*; for Chrift himfelf declared, that "*from the beginning it was not fo,*" Matt. xix 8, 9. and at the fame time our Lord informed the Jews, that " Mofes, becaufe " of *the hardnefs of their hearts,* fuffered " them to put away their wives."

NEITHER was it *according to the law of nature,* that the Jews were *permitted* in their behaviour and dealings, to make a partial diftinction between their

brethren

brethren of the houſe of Iſrael, and
ſtrangers. This national partiality was
not, indeed, either commanded or recommended in their law—but it was
clearly *permitted* or *tolerated,* and probably, for the ſame reaſon as the laſt
mentioned inſtance —" thou *ſhalt not*
" *lend* upon uſury to *thy brother*," &c.—
" unto *a ſtranger* thou mayeſt *lend upon*
" *uſury* &c. Deut. xxiii. 19.—Again---
" of *a foreigner* thou *mayeſt exaҁt* ;"
(that is, whatſoever *has been lent,* as appears by the preceding verſes) but that
which is, " thine, *with thy brother,*
" thine hand ſhall releaſe," Deut. xv. 3

Now all theſe laws were " *contrary
to the law of nature"* or " *natural equity,"* (whatever Mr. Thompſon, may
think) and were certainly, annulled or
rather *ſuperſeded,* as it were, by the
more perfeҁt doҁtrines of *univerſal benevolence* taught by Chriſt himſelf, who
" came

" came not to deftroy, but to fulfill the law."

In the law of Mofes we alfo read,
" Thou fhalt not avenge or bear grudge
" againſt *the children of thy people but*
" *thou ſhalt love thy neighbour as thy-*
" *felf,*" Leviticus xix. 18.

The Jews, accordingly, thought
themfelves fufficiently juſtified, if they
confined this glorious perfection of charity, viz. *the loving others as themfelves,*
to the perfons mentioned in the fame
verfe, viz. " *the children of their own*
" *people ;*" for they had no idea that fo
much love could poffibly be due to any
other fort of *neighbours* or *brethren.* But
Chriſt taught them by the parable of
the good Samaritan, that *all ſtrangers*
whatever even thofe who are declared
enemies, (as were the Samaritans to the
Jews) are to be efteemed our *neigh-*
bours

bours or *brethren,* whenever they ſtand
in need of our charitable aſſiſtance.

"THE Jewiſh inſtitution" indeed, as
Mr. Thompſon remarks " permited the
" uſe of *bondſervants,*" but did not permit the *bondage of brethren :* STRAN-
GERS ONLY could be *lawfully* retained as *bondmen*——" of the heathen,"
(or, more agreeable to the Hebrew
words, באת הגוים *of the nations*) " that
" are round about you; of *them* ſhall ye
" buy *bond* men and *bond* maids. More-
" over of the children of *ſtrangers* that
" do ſojourn among you, *of them ſhall*
" *ye buy,*" &c.----" *They* ſhall be your
" *bandmen for ever.*" Levit, xxv 39 to
46.

THIS was the law, I muſt acknowledge, with reſpect to *a ſtranger* that was
purchaſed ; but with reſpect to *a brother*

d   or

or Hebrew of the feed of Abraham, it was far otherwife, as the fame chapter teftifies ; (39th verfe) for, " if thy *bro-* ' *ther* that dwelleth by thee be waxen " poor, and be *fold* unto thee ; thou *fhalt* " *not compel him to ferve as a bondfervant:* " but as an hired fervant, and as a fo- " journer he fhall be with thee, and " fhall ferve thee unto the year of ju- " bilee. And *then fhall he depart from* " *thee, both he and his children with him,*" &c. This was the *utmoft fervitude* that a Hebrew could *lawfully* exact from a- ny of his *brethren* of the houfe of Ifrael, unlefs the fervant entered *voluntarily* into a perpetual fervitude : and, let me add, that it is alfo, the very *utmoft fervitude* that can *lawfully* be admitted *among chriftians:* becaufe we are bound as chriftians to efteem EVERY MAN *as our brother,* and *as our neighbour,* which I have already proved; fo that this confequence which

which I have drawn, is abfolutely *un-avoidable.* The Jews indeed, who do not yet acknowlege the commands of Chrift, may perhaps ftill think themfelves *juftified* by the law of Mofes, in making partial diftinctions between *their brethren* of Ifrael, *and other men* ? but it would *be inexcufable* in chriftians to do fo! and therefore I conclude, that we certainly have no right to exceed the *limits of fervitude,* which the Jews were bound to obferve, whenever their poor *brethren* were fold to them : and I apprehend that we muft not venture *even to go fo far,* becaufe the laws of *brotherly love* are infinitely enlarged, and extended by the gofpel of peace, which proclaims " *good will towards men,*" without diftinction ; and becaufe we cannot be faid to " *love our neighbours* " *as ourfelves ;*" or to *do to others as we would they fhould do unto us*"---whilft we

d 2   retain

retain them againſt their *will*, in a deſpicable ſervitude as *ſlaves*, and *private property*, or *mere chattels!*

THE glorious ſyſtem of the goſpel deſtroys all *narrow, national partiality*; and makes *us citizens of the world*, by obliging us to profeſs *univerſal benevolence :* but more eſpecially are we bound, as chriſtians, to commiſerate and aſſiſt to the utmoſt of our power all perſons in *diſtreſs,* or *captivity*; whatever " the " *worſhipful* committee of the compa- " ny of merchants trading to *Africa,*" may think of it, or their advocate, the reverend Mr. Thompſon.

CHARITY, indeed, begins at home ; and we ought moſt certainly to give the preference to our own countrymen, when ver we can do ſo without injuſtice ; but we may " *not do evil that* " *good*

" *good may come* ;" (though our ſtateſ-
men, and their political deceivers may
think otherwiſe) we muſt not, for the
ſake of *Old England*, and its *African
trade*, or for the ſuppoſed advantage,
or imaginary neceſſities of our *American*
colonies, lay aſide our *chriſtian charity,*
which we owe to *all the reſt of mankind :*
becauſe, *whenever we do ſo,* we certainly deſerve to be conſidered in no better
light than as an overgrown *ſociety of
robbers,* a *mere banditti,* who, perhaps, may *love one another,* but at the
ſame time are at enmity with *all the reſt
of the world.* Is this *according to the
law of nature* ?------For ſhame Mr.
Thompſon !

I ʜᴀᴠᴇ much more to communi-
cate, but no more time to write :---if I
had, I could draw from the ſcriptures
the

the moſt alarming examples of God's
ſevere judgments upon the Jews, for
tyrannizing over *their brethren,* and,
expreſsly, for exceeding the *limits* of
ſervitude juſt now mentioned. *(a)* I muſt
find time however to adopt one obſervation even from the reverend Mr. Thomp-
ſen, (p. 11.) viz. " This ſubjeƈt will
" grow more ſerious upon our hands,
" when we conſider the *buying and ſell-*
" *ing Negroes,* not as a clandeſtine or
" piratical buſineſs, but as an *open pub-*
" *lic trade,* *encouraged* and promoted by
" aƈts of parliament; for ſo, if being
" *contrary to religion, i t muſt be deemed* A
" NATIONAL SIN ; (*b*) and as ſuch may
" have

(a) This I have ſince accompliſhed in a traƈt, intituled, " THE LAW OF RETRIBUTION, &c.

(b) If this juſt remark by Mr. *Thompſon,* be compared with the above mentioned traƈt on *the Law of
Retribution,* (wherein the uſual courſe of God's judge:
ments

" have a confequence that *would be*
" *always to be dreaded.*" May God give
us grace to repent of this abominable
" NATIONAL SIN," before it is too late!
If I have vindicated the law of Mofes, much eafier can I vindicate the benevolent apoftle Paul, from Mr. Thompfon's infinuations, with refpect to flavery; for he *did not* entreat *Philemon* to
take back his fervant *Onefimus,* " in his
" former capacity," as Mr. *Thompfon*
has afferted, in order to render bondage " *confiftent with the principles of re-*
" *vealed religion,*"---but St. *Paul* faid
exprefly, " *not now as a fervant, but,*
" *above*

ments againft NATIONS, is fairly demonftrated by a
variety of unqueftionable examples in the fcriptures,)
it will appear that nothing but *a thorough reformation*
with refpect to the faid " NATIONAL SIN," can afford
us the leaft room *even to hope* that THIS NATION, may
efcape the tremendous effects of GODS TEMPORAL
VENGEANCE now dreadfully hanging over us!

" *above a servant*, a *brother beloved*," *(a)*
&c. So that Mr. *Thompson* has notori-
ously wrested St. *Paul*'s words.

In the other texts where St. *Paul*
recommends submiffion to *Servants*, for
confcience-fake, he at the fame time
enjoins the mafter to entertain fuch a
meafure of *brotherly love* towards his
fervants, as muft be entirely fubverfive
of the *African* trade, and *Weſt-Indian*
flavery.

(a) This fingle circumftance one would think a fufficient bar to the inferences drawn from this epiftle, in
favour of flavery, by the reverend Mr. *Thompson*, and
others ; and yet even the learned Archbifhop *Theophy-*
lact feemed inclined to admit the fame fuppofed *right*
of the mafter. In the preface to his commentary on
this epiftle, where he gives a fhort account of the ufe
and purport of it, and of the doctrines which may be
deduced from it, (he fays) Τριτον, ὁτι ὰ χρη προφαϭει
ευλαϭειας δαλας αποϭπαν των δεϭποτων μη βαλομενων.
Thirdly. That it is not fit, through pretence of piety, to
draw away fervants from mafters, that are unwilling to
part

flavery. And though St. *Paul,* recommends chriftian patience under fervitude, yet, at the fame time, he plainly infinuates, that it is inconfiftent with
e   chriftianity,

part with them." But though the apoftle declared, indeed, to *Philemon* the mafter, (v. 14.) " *without thy mind, would I do nothing* ;" &c. yet this by no means proves *the right of the mafter,* but only that the apoftle, in love and courtefy to *Philemon,* defired, that " *the benefit,*" which he required of him, " *fhould not be as it were of neceffity, but willingly,*" (ver. 14.) for the apoftle's *right* to have retained *Onefimus,* even without the ⸜mafter's confent,* is fufficiently implied in *a* preceding verfe, (viz. 8.) " *though I might be much bold in Chrift, to enjoin,* (or command) " *thee that which is convenient. Yet,* (faid the apoftle,) " *for* LOVE's SAKE, *I rather befeech.*" &c. And a further reafon for his not *commanding,* is alfo declared, viz. that he depended on the willing obedience of *Philemon.* " *Having confidence* (faid he) *in thy obedience, I wrote unto thee, knowing that thou wilt alfo do more than I fay.*" And yet that which he really did *fay,* or require in behalf of *Onefimus,* was as ftrong a recommendation

chriſtianity, and the dignity of Chriſt's
kingdom, that a *chriſtian brother* ſhould
be

mendation to *favour* and *ſuperior kindneſs* as could be
expreſſed. He required him to receive *Oneſimus*, " *not
now as a ſervant, but above a ſervant, as a* BROTHER
beloved," &c. (16 verſe.) that " *if he hath wronged thee,
or* OWETH OUGHT," (ἡ ὀφείλει, in which expreſſion
even the ſuppoſed *debt of ſervice* may be included,)
" *but that on my account,*" (ſaid the apoſtle, ver. 18.)
which muſt be a complete diſcharge of all the maſter's
temporal demands on *Oneſimus*; and therefore it is a
ſtrange perverſion of the apoſtle's meaning to cite this
epiſtle, *in favour of ſlavery,* when the whole tenor of
it is in behalf of the *ſlave!* But there is ſtill a further obſervation neceſſary to be made, which puts the
matter out of diſpute.

Theophylact, himſelf, allows that *Oneſimus* (at the very
time he was ſent back,) was *a miniſter of the goſpel,* or
a *miniſter of preaching* (Τȣ κηρυγματος, ‡) which is an
office

‡ αλλα παλιν αποςελει προς ὑπηρεσιαν τȣ κηρυγματος, ȣ
κ) αυτος εργατης εςι. But that he ſhould ſend him back again,
to the *ſervice* of *preaching,* of which he is *a labourer,* (or miniſter.) Comment on the 1ſt. verſe, page 863. edit. *London,*
1636.

be a *Slave*. " Can'ſt thou be made
" free ?" (ſays he to the chriſtian ſervants)
" *chooſe it rather*, for he that is *called*
" of the Lord, *being a ſervant*, is the
" *freeman* of the Lord ; and, in like
e 2 " manner,

office of the ſacred miniſtry, not beneath the higheſt
order in the church, for it was the principal employ-
ment even of the apoſtle himſelf.

And this opinion of *Theophylaƈt*, is corroborated by
a variety of circumſtances. By the epiſtle to the *Co-
loſſians*, it appears that *Oneſimus* was joined with *Tychicus*, (therein declared to be a *miniſter*,) ‖ in an *eccleſiaſ-
tical*

‖ ' *All my ſtate ſhall* TYCHICUS *declare* unto you, (who is) *a beloved brother*, A FAITHFUL MINISTER AND FELLOW SERVANT
' IN THE LORD ; *whom I have ſent unto you for the ſame purpoſe, that
' he might* KNOW YOUR ESTATE, AND COMFORT YOUR HEARTS
with ONESIMUS, *a faithful and beloved brother*," (by which it is
apparent that *Oneſimus* was joined in the ſame ſervices, " to KNOW
THEIR ESTATES AND COMFORT THEIR HEARTS," an office
that would have very ill become him, had he been ſent back to
his maſter as a SLAVE, or as Mr. *Thompſon* ſays ' IN HIS FORMER
' CAPACITY !)' " *who is one of you. They*(that is *Tychicus* and *Oneſimus*, jointly) *ſhall make known unto you all things which* (are done)
here." *Coloſſ* iv. 7. 9.

" manner, he that is called, *being free,*
" is the *fervant of Chrift,*"—" *Ye are*
" *bought with a price;* BE NOT THERE-
" FORE THE SERVANTS OF MEN."
The apoftle, indeed, had juft before
recom-

tical commiffion from the apoftle to the church of the
Coloffians, at the very time that he was fent back to
Philemon; § and it would furely have ill become the
apoftle to fend back *Onefimus,* then a *minifter of the gofpel,*
to ferve his mafter *Philemon, in his former capacity,*
(that is as a SLAVE) which is the doctrine prefumed in
page 18, of the reverend Mr. *Thompfon's* tract; Mr.
Thompfon, as a clergyman, ought to have confidered,
that this would not have been for the credit of the
gofpel miniftry. But *Onefimus* was not only a *minifter,* and
preacher, but afterwards even a *bifhop,* which will by
no means fuit with Mr. *Thompfon's* doctrine. The
learned bifhop *Fell,* teftified from the authority of *the
ancients,* that this *Onefimus* was a bifhop. " *Onefimus*"
fays

§ Ludov. Capellus, remarks that thefe epiftles, (viz. to *the Coloffians* and to *Philemon)* were wrote, (and confequently fent) at the fame
time, and after affigning feveral reafons for his opinion, concludes
as follows, " *Ex his itaque,* (fays he) *liquere puto utramque Epifto-
lam fimul eodem tempore fuiffe fcriptam.*" Hift. Apoft. illuft. page
79. ed *Genevæ,* 1634.

recommended to his difciples to *abide
in the fame calling,* wherein they were
called, and, " *being fervants, not to
care for it :*" That is, not to grieve
on account of *their temporal* ftate ; (for
if, inftead of thus enjoining *fubmiffion,*
he had abfolutely declared *the iniquity
of* SLAVERY, tho' *eftablifhed* and *au-
thoriz*ed by the laws of *temporal* govern-
ments, he would have occafioned more
tumult

(fays he in his commentary on Colloff. iv, 5) "*fervant
to Philemon, a chief man in Coloffe. The antients fay
that he fucceeded Timothy, in the* BISHOPRICK *of Ephe-
fus.*" And the great archbifhop *Ufher,* makes exprefs
mention of *Onefimus* in that *bifhoprick,* from the authority both of *Eufebius* and *Ignatius,* (fee his little
tract de. Epifcoporum et ἡ Metropolitanorum Ori-
gine, p. 9. ed. Lond. 1687.) So that though *Paul*
mentions to *Philemon* the receiving ONESIMUS FOR
EVER (*that thou fhouldeft receive him* FOR EVER." ver. 15)
yet it would be moft unreafonable to conceive that the
apoftle meant that he fhould receive him FOR EVER
AS A SLAVE ! The feveral circumftances I have mentioned, demonftrate the contrary.

tumult than *reformation* among the multitude of SLAVES, more ſtriving for *temporal* than *ſpiritual* happineſs ; yet it plainly appears, by the inſinuations, which immediately follow, that he thought it derogatory to the honour of chriſtianity, that men, *who " are " bought,"* with the ineſtimable *price of Chriſt's* blood, ſhould be eſteemed *ſervants* ; that is, *the Slaves,* and private property of other men ; and had chriſtianity been eſtabliſhed by *temporal* authority, in thoſe countries where *Paul* preached, as it is at preſent in theſe kingdoms, we need 'not doubt but that he would have *urged,* nay, compelled the maſters, *as he did Philemon,* by the moſt preſſing arguments, to treat their quondam ſlaves, " NOT " NOW AS SERVANTS, BUT ABOVE " SERVANTS----AS BRETHREN BE- " LOVED."

A N

A N

E L E G Y

On the miſerable STATE of an AFRICAN
SLAVE, by the celebrated and ingenious WILLIAM SHENSTONE, Eſq;

—SEE the poor native quit the Lybian ſhores,
   Ah ! not in love's delightful fetters bound !
No radiant ſmile his dying peace reſtores,
   Nor love, nor fame, nor friendſhip heals his wound.

Let vacant bards diſplay their boaſted woes,
   Shall I the mockery of grief diſplay ?
No, let the muſe his piercing pangs diſcloſe,
   Who bleeds and weeps his ſum of life away !

On the wild beach in mournful guiſe he ſtood,
   Ere the ſhril boatſwain gave the hated ſign ;
He dropt a tear unſeen into the flood ;
   He ſtole one ſecret moment, to repine.

Yet

Yet the mufe liften'd to the plaints he made;
  Such moving plaints as nature could infpire;
To me the mufe his tender plea convey'd,
  But fmooth'd, and fuited to the founding lyre.

" Why am I ravifh'd from my native ftrand?
  What favage race protects this impious gain?
Shall foreign plagues infeft this teeming land,
  And more than fea-born monfters plough the main?

Here the dire locufts horrid fwarms prevail;
  Here the blue afps with livid poifon fwell;
Here the dry dipfa wriths his finuous mail;
  O can we not here, fecure from envy, dwell?

When the grim lion urg'd his cruel chace,
  When the ftern panther fought his midnight prey,
What fate referv'd me for this chriftian race?
  O race more polifh'd, more fevere than they!

Ye prouling wolves purfue my lateft cries!
  Thou hungry tyger, leave thy reeking den!
Ye fandy waftes in rapid eddies rife!
  O tear me from the whips and fcorns of men!

Yet in their face fuperior beauty glows;
  Are fmiles the mein of rapine and of wrong?
Yet from their lip the voice of mercy flows,
  And ev'n religion dwells upon their tongue.

Of blifsful haunts they tell, and brighter climes,
  Where gentle minds convey'd by death repair,
But ftain'd with blood, and crimfon'd o'er with crimes
  Say, fhall they merit what they paint fo fair?

No, carelefs, hopelefs of thofe fertile plains,
  Rich by our toils. and by our forrows gay,
They ply our labours, and enhance our pains,
  And feign thefe diftant regions to repay.

For

For them our tufky elephant expires ;
　For them we drain the mine's embowel'd gold ;
Where rove the brutal nations wild defires ?—
　Our limbs are purchas'd, and our life is fold !

Yet fhores there are, bleft fhores for us remain,
　And favour'd ifles with golden fruitage crown'd,
Where tufted flow'rets paint the verdant plain.
　Where ev'ry breeze fhall med'cine ev'ry wound.

There the ftern tyrant that embitters life
　Shall vainly fuppliant, fpread his afking hand ;
There fhall we view the billow's raging ftrife,
　Aid the kind breaft, and waft his boat to land."

APPENDIX

(No. 2.)

Extract of a Letter from a Gentleman in *Maryland,* to his Friend in *London.*

' BUT whether I ſhall go thither or
' return home, I am yet undeter-
' mined; indeed, no where ſhall I ſtay
' long from England, for I had much ra-
' ther enjoy the bare neceſſaries of life
' there, than the moſt affluent circumſtan-
' ces in this country of moſt wretched Sla-
' very; which alone would render the life
' of any humane man moſt miſerable.
' There are four things under the Sun,
' which I equally abhor and abominate,
' viz. *Slavery* (under which I comprehend
' all cruelty, oppreſſion and injuſtice) and
' *licentiouſneſs, pride* and *impudence,* all
' which abound here in a monſtrous de-
' gree.
  ' The puniſhments of the poor negroes
' and convicts, are beyond all conception,
' being entirely ſubject to the will of their
' ſavage

' favage and brutal mafters, they are often
' punifhed for not doing more than ftrength
' and nature will admit of, and fometimes
' becaufe they can't on every occafion fall
' in with their wanton and capricious hu-
' mours. One common punifhment, is to
' flea their backs with cow hides, or other
' inftruments of barbarity, and then pour
' on hot rum, fuperinduced with brine
' or pickle, rub'd in with a corn hufk, in
' the fcorching heat of the Sun. For cer-
' tain, if your judges were fenfible of the
' fhocking treatment of the convicts here,
' they would hang every one of them, as
' an infinitely lefs punifhment, and tranf-
' port only thofe, whofe crimes deferve the
' fevereft death. Better be hanged *feven*
' hundred times, than ferve *feven* years
' here! and there is no redrefs, for magif-
' trates and all are equally interefted and
' criminal. If I had a child, I had rather
' fee him the humbleft fcavenger in the
' ftreets of *London*, than the loftieft ty-
' rant in *America*, with a thoufand flaves
' at his beck.'——

A P P E N D I X,

(N°. 3.)

A Letter from *Granville Sharp*, to *Jacob Bryant*, Efq; concerning the Defcent of the Negroes.

S I R,

' I Have conceived a very high opinion
' of your abilities, by perufing your
' learned account of *Egypt, and the Shep-*
' *herd Kings*, &c. and as you feem to have
' ftudied, very particularly, the hiftory of
' the *Cufeans* and antient *Arabians*, you
' can (I apprehend) eafily refolve fome
' doubts, relating thereto, which occurred
' to me on reading your book.

 ' I HAD always fuppofed that black men
' in general were defcended from *Cufh*, be-
' caufe a diftinction in colour from the reft
' of mankind, feems to have been particu-
' larly attributed to his defcendants, *the Cu-*
' *fhim*, even to a proverb.' " *Can the Cufhi*
" (commonly rendered Ethiopian) *change his*
" *Skin*," &c. (Jeremiah, xiii. 23.) and
 ' therefore

‘ therefore I concluded that all negroes,
‘ as well *Eaſt Indian* as *African*, are en-
‘ titled to the general name of *Cuſhim*,
‘ as being, probably, deſcended from dif-
‘ ferent branches of the ſame ſtock, be-
‘ cauſe the proverb is equally applicable to
‘ both, with reſpect to their complection,
‘ tho’ in many reſpects they are very dif-
‘ ferent. But in p. 254, of your learned
‘ work, where you are ſpeaking of the *Cu-*
‘ *ſeans* in general, you ſay, that they are
“ to be found within the tropics, almoſt
“ as low as the Gold coaſt,” &c. as if you
‘ apprehended, that the negroes on the
‘ Gold coaſt, and below it, *were not de-*
‘ *ſcended from Cuſh.*

‘ Now, Sir, I ſhall think myſelf greatly
‘ obliged, if you will be pleaſed to inform
‘ me, whether you really have any particu-
‘ lar reaſon to apprehend that the negroes
‘ on the coaſt of *Guinea* (from whence our
‘ plantations are moſt commonly ſupplied)
‘ are deſcended from any other ſtock? Or
‘ whether their deſcent can at all be traced?

‘ I am far from having any particular
‘ eſteem for the negroes, but as I think
‘ myſelf *obliged* to conſider them as *Men*,
‘ I am certainly *obliged*, alſo, to uſe my beſt
‘ endeavours to prevent their being treated
‘ *as beaſts*, by our unchriſtian countrymen,
‘ who deny them the privileges of *human*
‘ *Nature*; and, in order to excuſe their
‘ own

' own *brutality*, will fcarcely allow that
' negroes are *human Beings*.

' THE tracing their defcent, therefore,
' is a point of fome confequence to the
' fubject, in which I am now engaged for
' their defence.'   *   *   *   *

I am,

SIR,

Your moft obedient,

Old *Jewry*,
19*th* O&r. 1772.   humble Servant,

GRANVILLE, SHARP.

JACOB BRYANT, Efq;

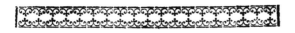

APPENDIX

(No. 4.)

Mr. *Bryant's* Anfwer to the foregoing Letter.

Cypenham, 20*th* O&r. 1772.

S I R,

' I MOST fincerely wifh you fuccefs in
' your laudable purpofe : and am very
' glad to find in thefe bafe times, that there
' is a perfon, who will ftand up in defence
' of human nature ; and not fuffer it to be
' limited to a fet of features and complexion.
' There is nothing, I believe, in my wri-
' tings, that can affect any argument,
' which you may think proper to urge in
' favour of thofe, whom you would patro-
' nize. But to take away all embarraf-
' ment, and uncertainty, I will give you
' my opinion upon the fubject, which you
' have ftated to me in your letter, in
' refpect to the origin of the Nigritæ or
' Negroes. You feem to think, that all,
' who are of that very deep tint, which is
' obfervable

' obfervable in the natives upon the coaft
' of Guinea, are the offspring of *Chus*:
' and all black men in general are of the
' fame origin. To this I take the liberty
' to anfwer, that all the natives of *Africa*
' are more or lefs fwart: and even among
' the negroes there are a great variety of
' tints, from a light copper colour to the
' darkeft black. All the inhabitants of
' this vaft continent are affuredly the fons of
' *Ham*: but not equally dercended from
' *Chus*. For though his pofterity was very
' dark, yet many of the collateral branches
' were of as deep a die: and *Africa* was
' peopled from *Ham*, by more families
' than one. It was poffeffed by fome of
' them, as there is good grounds to fur-
' mife, before the *Cufhites* came into *Egypt*.
' We learn from fcripture, that *Ham* had
' four fons, *Chus*, *Mizraim*, *Phut* and *Ca-*
' *naan*, Gen. x. v. 6. *Canaan* occupied
' *Paleftine*, and the country called by his
' his name: *Mizraim Egypt*: But *Phut*
' paffed deep into *Africa*, and, I believe,
' moft of the nations in that part of the
' world are defcended from him: at leaft
' more than from any other perfon.
' *Jofephus* fays, " *that Phut was the foun-*
" *der of the nations in Libya,* * *and the*
" *people*

* See Jofephus, Antq. lib. 1 c. 7.

" *people were from him called,* (Φυτοι)
" *Phuti.*" By *Libya* he underſtands, as the
' *Greeks* did, *Africa* in general : for the
' particular country, called *Libya* proper,
' was peopled by the *Lubim,* or *Lehabim,*
' one of the branches from *Mizraim,* Λαϭιειμ
' ϳξ ὁυ Λιϭυες. Chron. Paſchale, p. 29.

' THE ſons of *Phut,* ſettled in *Maurita-*
' *nia,* where was a country called *Phutia,*
' and a river of the like denomination.
" Mauritaniæ Fluvius uſque ad præſens
" tempus *Phut* dicitur, omniſque circa
" eum regio *Phutenſis.* (Hieron͛. Tradit.
" Hebrææ.) —— Amnem, quem vocant
" *Fut :*" (Pliny, lib. 5. c. i.)—Some of this
' family ſettled above Egypt, near Æthi-
' opia, and were ſtiled Troglodytæ.   Φουδ
' εξ ὁυ Τρωγλοδυται   Syncellus, p. 47.
' Many of them paſſed inland, and peopled
' the *Mediterranean* country. In proceſs of
' time, (after their expulſion from *Egypt,)*
' the ſons of *Chus* made ſettlements upon
' the ſea coaſt of *Africa,* and came into
' *Mauritania.* Hence we find traces of
' them alſo in the names of places, ſuch as
' *Churis, Chuſares,* upon the coaſt : and a
' river *Cuſa,* and a city *Cotta,* together
' with a promontory *Cotis* in *Mauritania,*
' all denominated from *Chus* ; who at dif-
' ferent times and by different people was
' called *Chus,* **Cuth,** *Coſh* and *Cotis.* The
' river *Cuſa* is mentioned by *Pliny,* lib. 5.

' c. 1. and by *Ptolomey.* Many ages after
' thefe fettlements, there was another ir-
' ruption of the *Cuſhites* into thefe parts,
' under the name of *Saracens* * and *Moors* ;
' who over ran *Africa,* to the very extre-
' mities of mount *Atlas.* They paffed
' over, and conquered *Spain* to the north :
' and they extended themfelves fouthward,
' as I faid in my treatife, to the rivers *Sene-*
' *gal* and *Gambia,* and as low as the *Gold*
' *Coaſt.* I mentioned this, becaufe I do
' not think, that they proceeded much far-
' ther : moſt of the nations to the fouth
' being, as I imagine, of the race of *Phut.*
' The very country upon the river *Gambia*
' on one fide, is at this day called *Phuta,* of
' of which *bluet,* in his hiſtory of *Juba Ben*
' *Solomon,* gives an account,

' It is not poſſible to difcriminate at this
' æra of time the feveral caſts among the
' black nations, but I ſhould think, that
' we may be pretty certain, that they were
' not all *Cuſhim,* or *Cuſeans.* The Negroes
' are woolly headed ; and fo were fome of
' the *Æthiopes* or *Cuſhim* : but nothing can
' be inferred from this : for many of the
' latter had long hair, as we learn from *He-*
' *rodotus,* lib. 7. c. 70. ιθυτριχες. We
' find

* *Query* --Whether the *Saracens* may not rather be
faid to be of the line of *Shem,* as being defcended
from *Abraham* ?—Though indeed, both the mother
and the wife of *Iſhmael,* were *Egyptians.*

' find from *Marcellinus*, that the *Egyp-*
' *tians* were *Crifpi*, and had a tendency to
' woolly hair : fo that this circumftaice can-
' not always be looked upon as a family
' characteriftic.

' THIS, Sir, is my opinion concerning
' the people in queftion, which I fubmit to
' your confideration, merely as matter of
' opinion : for I cannot pretend to fpeak
' with certainty. It makes very little dif-
' ference in refpect to tne good caufe,
' which your humanity prompts you to ef-
' poufe, whether the Nigritæ are *Phutians*,
' or *Cufhites*. They are certainly the fons
' of *Ham* : and, what is more to the pur-
' pofe, they are the workmanfhip of God,
' formed in his image witn a living Soul ;
' as well as ourfelves. Confequently they
' deferve better treatment, than they have
' generally experienced from thofe, who
' look upon themfelves, as more enlighten-
' ed, and poffeffed of a greater degree of
' humanity. I join with you fincerely in
' detefting the cruel traffic : and am, with
' great truth,   S I R,

Your moft obedient,

and moft humble Servant,

JACOB BRYANT.

' P. S. You are pleafed to obferve, *that*
' *a diftinction in colour from the reft of man-*
kind

' kind feems to have been particularly attri-
' buted to the defcendants of the Cufhim. They
' certainly were very dark : but fo were all
' the fons of Ham. And it is difficult to
' fay, who were the darkeft, as it was a
' circumftance depending upon the fituation
' of the people fpoken of, and upon many
' occult caufes. The fame family in differ-
' ent parts varied from itfelf, as I have fhewn
' from Herodotus. The facred writers fpeak
' of the Cufhi's complexion particularly, be-
' caufe they were moft acquainted with it,
' as being very near Shem. There were fe-
' veral regions, called Cufhan or Æthiopia,
' one of which was upon the confines of
' Judæa, near Amalec and Edom ; but ftill
' nearer to Midian. Hence the prophet
' Habbakuh fays in a vifion,—" I faw the
" tents of Cufhan in affliction, and the cur-
" tains of Midian did tremble." C. iii. v. 7.
' Thefe were the Araba Cufhitæ; with
' whom the Ifraelites were moft acquainted.
' Of the fons of Phut, and of the Ludim,
' Lehabim, and other defcendants of Ham,
' in Africa, they had probably little or no
' cognizance, excepting only the Mizraim,
' and the Æthiopians immediately above
' them to the fouth of Syene. With thefe
' they were acquainted. Should it be in
' my power to give you any farther fatisfac-
' tion, I fhall be very proud of your com-
' mands. * * * * *

'THE

' THE whole of what you mention, that
' all Moors, Negroes, and black perfons are
' from one common ftock is moft affuredly
' true, if you make the head of that family
' *Ham*, inftead of *Chus*. One remove higher
' makes every thing ftrictly confonant to
' the truth.'

A P P E N D I X

(No. 5.)

The Regulations lately adopted by th
Spaniards, at the *Havanna,* and fom
other Places, for the gradual *enfran
chifement of Slaves,* are to the follow
ing Effect.

' AS foon as a flave is landed, hi
' name, price, &c. are regiftered i
' a public regifter ; and the mafter is oblig
' ed, by law, to allow him *one working da*
' in every week, to himfelf, *befides Sundays*
' fo that, if the flave chufes to work for hi
' mafter on that day, he receives the *wage*
' *of a freeman* for it ; and whatever he gain
' by his labour, on that day, is fo fecured t
' him by law, that the mafter cannot de
' prive him of it. This is certainly a con
' fiderable ftep towards the abolifhing *abfo*
' *lute flavery.* As foon as the flave is abl
' to purchafe *another working day,* the maf
' ter is obliged to fell it to him at a propor
' tionable price, *viz.* one fifth part of hi
' origin

‘ original coft ; and fo, likewife, the re-
‘ maining four days, at the fame rate, as
‘ foon as the flave is able to redeem them ;
‘ after which *he is abfolutely free*: This is
‘ fuch encouragement to induftry, that even
‘ the moft indolent are tempted to exert
‘ themfelves. Men, who have thus work-
‘ ed out their freedom, are enured to the
‘ labour of the country, and are certainly
‘ the moft ufeful fubjects that a colony can
‘ acquire. Regulations might be formed
‘ upon the fame plan to encourage the in-
‘ duftry of flaves *that are already imported*
‘ *into the colonies*, which would teach them
‘ how to maintain themfelves, and be *as*
‘ *ufeful*, as well as *lefs* expenfive to the plan-
‘ ter. They would by fuch means become
‘ members of fociety, and have an intereft
‘ in the welfare of the community ; which
‘ would add greatly to the ftrength and fe-
‘ curity of each colony : whereas, at pre-
‘ fent, many of the plantations are in *conti-*
‘ *nual danger of being cut off by their flaves*,
‘ a fate which they but *too juftly deferve*.’

APPEN

A P P E N D I X,

(No. 6.)

Extract of a Letter from the Author,
to a Gentleman at *Philadelphia*.

'———— and furely there needs no argu-
' ment to demonftrate the weaknefs and dan-
' ger of the more fouthern colonies, from *the*
' *immenfe multitude of flaves*, that are forci-
' bly detained therein !

' THE congrefs have acted nobly in for-
' bidding the iniquitous importation of *more*
' *flaves*; but the bufinefs is but half done,
' 'till they have agreed upon fome equitable
' and fafe means of *gradually enfranchifing*
' thofe which remain. No time fhould be
' loft in forwarding this equitable meafure ;
' —and, to fecure the affections of the ne-
' groes, affurances fhould be immediately
' given of fuch friendly intentions towards
' them, left any attack fhould, in the mean
' while, be made in thofe quarters, which
might

' might encourage *an infurrection*. I tremble
' for the probable confequences of fuch an
' event ! for though *domeftic flavery;* (which
' I deteft from my heart) would thereby be
' abolifhed, yet that effect would be wrought
' at the expence of *public Liberty ;* and the
' *tyranny* and injuftice of private individuals
' would feem, perhaps, to be too feverely
' punifhed by that horrid carnage and im-
' placability, which ufually attend the con-
' flicts between mafters and flaves !

  ' LET *private intereft* therefore give place
' to *juftice* and *right*, which will moft effec-
' tually adminifter to the public fafety.

  ' LET it be remembered that many of
' the negroes are natives of the colonies,
' and confequently have *a natural right* to a
' *free exiftence* therein, as well as the Land-
' holders themfelves. I fhall not prefume
' to *advife* the mode of effecting this im-
' portant and neceffary enfranchifement,
' but will only offer a few hints in order to
' promote the confideration and determina-
' tion of thofe who are beft able to judge
' of the matter.

  ' SUPPOSE the value of every flave now in
' the colonies, was to be fairly eftimated, by
' juries appointed for that purpofe, and the
' value to be entered, under their infpection,
' (as a pecuniary *debt* due from each negroe
' to his mafter,) in a public regifter for each
' diftrict. Suppofe alo that the landholders,

'who do not occupy all their grounds, were
'advised to divide what lands they can spare
'into *compact little farms*, with a small wooden
'cottage to each, which should be allotted
'to those negroes only, who are natives of
'the colony, or else have been so long in it,
'that their dispositions are sufficiently known,
'whether or not they may safely be entrust-
'ed with their liberty. Let such negroes hold
'these small portions of land by leases, for
'a certain term of years ; and at equitable
'rents, to be paid in such portions of *the*
'*produce* from time to time, as shall be
'thought most reasonable, leaving the ten-
'ants a moderate gain, (besides their necef-
'fary subsistence) to encourage industry, and
'yet so as to yield the landlords a due profit
'from each portion of their estates, besides
'an adequate allowance to reimburse (within
'the limited time) not only the registered
'price of their quondam slaves, but, also
'whatever sums they may have advanced to-
'wards the expence of *building*, of *implements*,
'of *live stock*, of *seed*, &c. &c. the amount
'of which ought to be added to the first
'debt and registered, in like manner, before
'the leases are executed. By these means the
'landlords will lose nothing of their wealth,
'and yet the most useful and worthiest of the
'negroes will acquire a *natural interest* in
'the welfare and safety of the community,
'which will insure their assistance against
                                            'any

' any hoftile attempt of the reft.   Other
' negroes, that are not capable of managing
' and fhifting for themfelves, nor are fit to be
' trufted, all at once, with liberty, might be
' delivered over to the care and protection of
' a county committee, in order to avoid the
' baneful effects of *private property in men*;
' and might, by the faid committee, be let
' out, as *hired fervants*, to fuch perfons as
' would undertake the charge of them, to
' be paid (alfo *in produce*) towards' the dif-
' charge of the regiftered debt for each
' man's original price ; and the labourer
' himfelf in the mean while to be allow-
' ed one day in a week (befide the Sun-
' day for his own profit, or be paid
' for it according to the mode of the
' *Spanifh regulations*, (which I before tranf-
' mitted) that he may have an opportuni-
' ty to acquire a little property of his own,
' which will *prepare his mind*, as well as
' his circumftances *for freedom*, by enabling
' him, as a member of the community to
' fhift for himfelf at the time of his dif-
' charge.   By fome fuch regulations, as
' thefe, flavery might be changed into a
' condition, more nearly refembling that of
' *hired fervants*, as no mafter would be the
' *abfolute proprietor* of thofe he employs,
' and yet all reafonable advantages arifing
' from their labour, would remain ; which
' muft occafion a reciprocal improvement
' in the morality and humanity both of maf-

' ters and fervants; and in procefs of time,
' inftead of *wretched flaves*, a new and ufe-
' ful órder of men, at prefent unknown in
' America, (where every *freeman* cultivates
' his own ground only) would be eftablifhed
' amongft you; I mean a hardy body of
' *free peafants*, ferving either as *trufty ten-*
' *ants* or *farmers*, to improve thereftates of
' landed gentlemen, or elfe as *laboriòus cot-*
' *tagers*, who might be employed with in-
' finite advantage to the neighbourhood,
' wherever eftablifhed, efpecially if they
' were encouraged by an allotment of a
' fmall patch of land for a potatoe ground
' or garden, with a right of pafture for a
' little live ftock upon fome common field
' in the neighbourhood of their little cot-
' tages. — Landholders by this means would
' have their eftates better peopled and im-
' proved, and yet avoid the guilt and dan-
' ger of oppreffion.   In the mean while, the
' hours of labour fhould be uniformly regu-
' lated, to prevent the oppreffion of avari-
' cious exactors, and the danger of difcon-
' tent: and fchools fhould be opened in
' every diftrict, to give the poor labourers
' and their children, fome general ideas of
' morality and, religious knowledge, which
' conftitute the moft effectual *bond of peace.*
' Thefe regulations I mention only by way
' of hint : you have the fame earneft regard
' for

' for the caufe of *general liberty*, and *the*
' *natural rights of mankind* that I have,
' and much greater abilities to defend them,
' and to propofe a more perfect fyftem than
' what is here fuggefted.   Let me therefore
' intreat you to confider this matter, and to
' forward, as foon as poffible, fome fcheme
' of general enfranchifement, becaufe Ame-
' rican liberty cannot be firmly eftablifhed
' 'till this is done.

' I am with great efteem,

'Dear S I R,

' Your affectionate friend

and humble fervant.'

London,
18 July, 1775.

'GRANVILLE SHARP.'

APPENDIX,

(No. 7.)

Extract from Mr *Morgan*'s Book, intituled, ' *A Plan for the Abolition of*
' *Slavery, in the West Indies.*'

—Page 12.——' Nothing can be more
' oppofite to every idea of juftice and mo-
' rality than the prefent practice of buying
' flaves, to cultivate the Weft Indian iflands
' and the fouthern provinces on the conti-
' nent of America ; nor can any thing, I
' *think, be eventually more fatal* — * * *

Page 13.——' Yet fomething, out of
' worldly prudence, ought to be done ;—for,
' as this evil has been violently introduced,
' contrary to the natural courfe of things
' and the conftitution of the world, it will
' one day find a remedy even in its excefs.
' Matters will be fatally brought to a crifis,
' and nature will vindicate her own laws,
' and

' and reftore the credit of her equal and
' juft adminiftration, to the lafting punifh-
' ment of thofe who abufed it. THIS WILL
' BE WHEN THE BLACKS OF THE SOUTH-
' THERN COLONIES ON THE CONTINENT
' OF AMERICA SHALL BE NUMEROUS
' ENOUGH TO THROW OFF AT ONCE THE
' YOKE OF TYRANNY TO REVENGE THEIR
' WRONGS IN THE BLOOD OF THEIR OP-
' PRESSORS, AND CARRY TERROR AND
' DESTRUCTION TO THE MORE NORTHERN
' SETTLEMENTS. Such a revolution can-
' not take place in the iflands until this
' period, on account of the want of intel-
' ligence and communication between the
' flaves of one ifland and another, and of
' the ea'y communication and mutual af-
' fiftance of whites. But an infurrection on
' the continent, once communicated, will
' be an incitement in the iflands, and a fig-
' nal for a general and (but that every
' Englifhman is alike concerned, and the
' planter not peculiarly criminal) A MERIT-
' ED CARNAGE.
  ' Nothing can be conceived MORE DE-
' STRUCTIVE, MORE INSATIATE, THAN
' THE WARS WHICH WILL FOLLOW THIS
' EVENT ; they will be every where marked
' with THE MOST HORRIBLE CRUELTIES,
' and THE MOST FURIOUS REVENGE. The
' diftinction of *black* and *white*, which we
                                        ' have

' have fo unreafonably made the marks of
' *freedom* and *flavery*, will then become
' the obvious colours of mutual hoftility and
' revenge; and it feems likely that thefe
' wars MAY END TO THE DISADVANTAGE
' OF THE WHITES; becaufe the blacks, as will
' be prefently obferved, will increafe fafter,
' and becaufe their nature feems better able
' to bear the feverity of cold, than the
' whites can that of heat.'—*&c.*

APPEN-

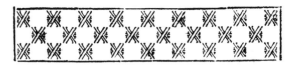

A P P E N D I X,

(No 8.)

A Copy of what " *is faid* to be the
" fubftance of Lord *Mansfield*'s fpeech
" in the cafe of *Somerfet* and *Knowles :*"

ON Monday the 22d June, in Trinity
term, 1772, the court of *King*'s
Bench, proceeded to give judgement in the
Cafe of *Somerfet* and *Knowles*, upon the return of the Habeas Corpus. LORD MANS-
FIELD firft ftated the return; and then
fpoke to the following purport, which is
taken from the fecond edition of a Tract,
printed in 1773, intituled, " *Confidera-*
" *tions on the Negroe Caufe, fo called, ad-*
" *dreffed to the right honourable lord* Mans-
" field, *lord chief juftice of the court of*
" *King's Bench, by* SAMUEL ESTWICK,
" *A. M. Affiftant Agent for the ifland of*
" Barbadoes." page vii. *viz.*

' WE pay due attention to the opinion
' of Sir *Philip Yorke* and Mr. *Talbot*, in
' the year 1729, by which they pledged
' themfelves to the Britifh planters for the

i   ' legal

‘ legal confequences of bringing Negroe-flaves
‘ into this kingdom, or their being baptiz-
‘ ed ; which opinion was repeated and re-
‘ cogniz d by lord Hardwicke, fitting as
‘ chancellor, on the 19th of October, 1749,
‘ to the following effect : he faid,’ “ that
“ trover would'lay for a negroe-flave : that a
“ notion prevailed, that if a flave came into
“ England, or became a Chriftian, he there-
“ by became emancipated ; but there was no
“ foundation in law for fuch a notion : that
“ when he and Lord Talbot were attorney
“ and folicitor general, this notion of a flave
“ becoming free by being baptized per-
“ vailed fo ftrongly, that the planters induf-
“ trioufly prevented their becoming chrif-
“ tians : upon which their opinion was taken ;
“ *and upon their beft confideration they were*
“ *both clearly of opinion*, that a flave did not
“ in the leaft alter his fituation or ftate to-
“ wards his mafter or *owner*, either by be-
“ ing chriftened, or coming to England :
“ that though the ftatute of Charles II. had
“ abolifhed” *(homage ‡)* “ tenure fo far,
“ that no man could be a *Villein regardant* ;
“ yet if he would acknowledge himfelf a
“ *Villein* engroffed in any court of record, he
‘ knew

(‡) See a part of my lord *Mansfield's* fpeech printed
in the Appendix, (p. 11.) of “ *a Treatife upon the*
“ *Trade from* Great Britain *to* Africa, *by an African*
“ *merchant*,” wherein this word “ *homage*” is inferted.

" knew of no way by which he could be en-
" titled to his freedom, without the confent
" of his mafter." ' We feel the force of
' the inconveniences and confequences that
' will follow the decifion of this queftion :
' yet all of us are fo clearly of one opinion
' upon the *only* queftion before us, that we
' think we ought to give judgment without
' adjourning the matter to be argued before
' all the judges, as ufual in the habeas cor-
' pus, and as we at firft intimated an inten-
' tion of doing in this cafe. The only quef-
' tion then is, *Is the caufe returned fufficient*
' *for the remanding him ?* *If not*, he muft be
' difcharged. The caufe returned is, the
' *flave* abfented himfelf and departed from
' his mafter's fervice, and refufed to return
' and ferve him during his ftay in *England* ;
' whereupon, by his mafter's orders, he was
' put on board the fhip by force, and there
' detained in fecure cuftody, to be carried
' out of the kingdom and fold. So hi h
' an act of dominion muft derive its autho-
' rity, if any fuch it has, from the law of
' the kingdom *where* executed. A foreig-
' ner cannot be imprifoned *here* on the au-
' thority of any law exifting in his own coun-
' try. The power of a mafter over his fer-
' vant is different in all countries, more or
' lefs limited or extenfive , the exercife of
' of it therefore muft always be regulated

' by the laws of the place where exercifed.
' The ftate of flavery is of fuch a nature,
' that it is incapable of being now, intro-
' duced by courts of juftice upon mere rea-
' foning, or inferences from any principles
' natural or political; it muft take its rife
' from *pofitive law*; the origin of it can in
' no country or age be traced back to any
' other fource. Immemorial ufage preferves
' the memory of *pofitive law* long after all
' traces of the occafion, reafon, authority,
' and time of its introduction, are loft, and
' in a CASE SO ODIOUS AS THE CONDITION
' OF SLAVES MUST BE TAKEN STRICTLY.
' *(Tracing the fubject to natural princi-*
' *ples, the claim of flavery never can be fup-*
' *ported.)* (‡) THE POWER CLAIMED BY
' THIS RETURN WAS NEVER IN USE
' HERE: (or *acknowledged by the law.)* No
' mafter ever was allowed here to take a
' flave by force to be fold abroad becaufe he
' had deferted from his fervice, or for any
' other reafon whatever; WE CANNOT SAY,
' *the caufe fet forth by this return* IS ALLOW-

I 2   ' ED

(‡) Thefe additions in Italics between hooks before
and after the words " THE POWER CLAIMED BY
THIS RETURN WAS NEVER IN USE HERE," are
taken from the notes of a very ingenious and able
counfellor, who was prefent when the judgement
was given.—The reft of his notes fufficiently agree
in fubftance with what Mr. *Eftwick* has printed.

' ED OR APPROVED OF BY THE LAWS OF
' THIS KINGDOM, and therefore the man
' muſt be diſcharged.'

Upon this Mr. *Eſtwick* has been pleaſed
to obſerve as follows, ' *I muſt confeſs* (ſays he)
' *I have been greatly puzzled in endeavouring*
' *to reconcile this judgement with this ſtate of*
' *it, and with my comprehenſion,*' &c. But the
writer quoted by the *African merchant* before
mentioned, is not ſo modeſt in his cenſure
of this judgement, nor ſo honeſt in his *re-
cital* of it, as Mr. *Eſtwick*, for he partially
conceals the moſt material part of the learned judge's ſpeech, becauſe it happens to
make againſt his own wicked cauſe ; and
tells us by way of excuſe for ſo notorious
and partial an omſſion—that " *the remain-*
' *der of the ſpeech is too vague to come into*
' *conſideration,*' &c. (p. 12.) Another anonymous writer (author of a pamphlet, intitled
' CANDID REFLECTIONS *upon* THE JUDGE-
' MENT *lately awarded by the Court of King's*
' *Bench, in Weſtminſter Hall, on what is com-*
' *monly* called the NEGROE CAUSE, *by a Plan-*
' *ter,*') after comparing this JUDGEMENT
of the King's Bench, with the opinions of the
judges *Holt* and *Powel,* and thoſe of the
attorney and ſolicitor general, *York* and *Talbot,* &c. is pleaſed to *reflect* thereupon as
follows. " *A point,* (ſays he) *upon which*
" *theſe great Oracles of the law have publiſhed*
" *ſuch*

" *ſuch oppoſite ſentiments, ſeems as far as ever*
" *from being eſtabliſhed upon the ſolid ground of*
" *abſolute* PRECISION. *The planters of courſe*
" *have been left* (ſays he) *as much puzzled*
" *by this* DELPHIC AMBIGUITY, *as the ſages*
" *themſelves appear to have been, in forming*
" *their judgements upon the ſubjeĉt. The mat-*
" *ter having been* CONFOUNDED *in this*
" GRAND UNCERTAINTY," &c. (p. 57.)
But theſe heavy charges of the want of
" PRECISION, ' of " DELPHIC AMBIGUITY,"
and of being " CONFOUNDED in GRAND UN-
"CERTAINTY," &c. are ſo far from being
" CANDID REFLECTIONS," (as this author
would have us believe them,) that even *his
own evidence* on the preceeding page, clearly proves the falſehood and injuſtice of his
cenſures ; for he has there given us the
EFFECT of that late judgment of the court
of King's Bench, in THE CLEAREST TERMS,
without the leaſt *doubt*,or *difficulty* ; ſo that
the *delphic ambiguity*, of which he *immediately after* complains, muſt be (even according to his own evidence,) a mere *calumny* !
    After reciting the opinion of lord chief
juſtice *Holt*, he immediately adds as follows.
    " *Lord chief juſtice* mansfield (ſays he)
" *adds to this effeĉt.*
    " That the laws of *Great Britain* do not
" authorize a maſter to *reclaim* his fugi-
" tive SLAVE, *confine* or *tranſport* him out of
" the kingdom. In other words;" (ſays
                                        he)

he) " that a negroe flave, coming from the
" colonies into *Great Britain* becomes, *ipfo*
" *faƈto*, FREE."

Thus, notwithftanding the *un-candid re-
fleƈtions* of this author about DELPHIC AM-
BIGUITY, yet even *he himfelf* has without
doubt or *difficulty*, declared THE *certain* and
unavoidable EFFECT of the judgement delivered by Lord *Mansfield!* That this author (notwithftanding his prejudices, and
unjuft cenfures about ambiguity) has really ftated the *certain* and *unavoidable* EFFECT
of the faid judgment, will appear by the
following remarks upon it.

A P P E N D I X

(No. 9.)

Remarks on the Judgment of the Court
of *King's Bench*, in the Cafe of
Stewart and *Somerfet*. By *Granville Sharp*.

THIS judgment will not appear doubtful and inexplicit, (as fome have too
haftily efteemed it) if the whole be taken
together, and THE EFFECT of it be duly
confidered.

LORD *Mansfield* pronounced the fenti-
ments or judgment *of the whole bench*, and
therefore if any thing was wrong, the
blame ought not to reft on him alone ; neverthelefs, if we fairly examine what was
faid, we fhall find no room for blame or
cavil, His lordfhip faid, " WE *pay due*
' *attention* to the opinion of Sir *Philip*
' *York* and Mr. *Talbot*, in the year 1729,'

Now

Now the purport of that opinion was, that the mafter ' *may legally compel* his flave ' *to return to the plantations.*'

LORD *Mansfield* modeltly declined giving a direct contradiction, in exprefs words, to the opinion of two fuch very eminent and learned lawyers; but chofe rather to condemn it, tacitly, by *the effect* of the judgment, which he was about to pronounce ; and therefore he merely recited the opinion without the leaft comment, and proceeded to the determination of the court upon the cafe before them ; which is clear and incontrovertible with refpect to the main point of the queftion, viz. the power claimed by the mafter, of carrying away his flave by force.

' *The power claimed by this return,* (faid the ' chief juftice) *was never in ufe here, or ac-* ' *knowledged by the law.*' Now it was certainly the duty of the court to give judgment according to *the known laws*, and not to be influenced by *any opinion* whatfoever.

THEY acknowledged, indeed, the having " *paid due attention*" to the faid opinion ; but as their determination was diametrically oppofite to the affertions in that opinion, it is manifelt, that the court *did not think it grounded in law*, according to which alone they were bound to determine. The conclufion of lord *Mansfield*'s fpeech contains

k   more

more fubftantial and unanfwerable reafons
for the judgment he was about to give, than
the generality of his hearers, perhaps, were
aware of ; for he very ingenioufly expreffed
in the fmall compafs of two fhort fentences,
that the mafters claim was contrary to
three principal foundations of the English
law, viz. NATURE, USE, (or Custom,) and
the WRITTEN LAW; which laft alfo includes
two other foundations, viz. MAXIMS and
STATUTES. With refpect to the firft, he faid
— " traceing the fubject to NATURAL princi-
" ples, the claim of SLAVERY never can be
" fupported." With refpect to the fecond, he
faid, — " The power claimed by this return was
" never in USE here," and thirdly, that it was
" never acknowledged by THE LAW."

THESE feem to have been the reafons of
the determination ; and confequently the
court was obliged by the common law
(which always favours, LIBERTY) ‖ to difcharge the man from the unnatural and un-
precedented claims of his matter, which was
accordingly done, fo that the true meaning
of this determination is rendered clear and
incontrovertible, as well by the effect of it,
as by the unanfwerable reafons above mentioned.

THAT

‖ ' Law favoureth life, LIBERTY, and DOWER.'
' Law regards the PERSON above his poffeffions, – LIFE
' and LIBERTY, moft,' &c. (Principia Legis et Æquit.
P. 56.
LIBERTAS eft res ineftimablis.' (Jenk. Cent. 52.)

THAT there is nothing *doubtful* or *inexplicit* in this *judgment*, de ivered bv lord *Mansfield,* will further appear by the following report of a cafe in the PREROGATIVE COURT, wherein this very determination on *Somerfet's* cafe, is exprefsly cited, and the EFFECT of it clearly and fully declared by a learned judge of that court. And the propriety of the faid judgment has very lately been ftill further confirmed by a decree alfo in THE HIGH COURT OF ADMIRALTY, after a very learned and folemn debate concerning the *legality,* or, *illegality* of *flavery* in *England,* wherein the merits of the queftion on both fides was fully examined and difcuffed. A fhort ftate of the Cafe, together with the fubftance of the decree will be found in Appendix, No. 11. The offence expreffed in this latter Cafe was fo flagrantly wicked in all its circumftances, and upon the whole, was fo notorious a contempt of the laws and conftitution of this kingdom, as well as of *natural right,* and common honefty, that all perfons, who have any regard for juftice, muft be moved with indignation againft the authors of the mifchief, and muft wifh to fee them corrected by fome *adequate* and *exemplary punifhment,* inftead of a decifion againft them for the mere *recovery of wages.* In order therefore to prevent any unjuft prejudice of well meaning people, againft the manner of proceeding in this cafe for redrefs, it is ne-

ceffary

ceffary to remark, that the negroe did not
' *apply for redrefs of thefe injuries,*' till more
than two years after they were committed,
whereby he was deprived of the *fatisfaction*
to which THE HABEAS CORPUS ACT would
otherwife have entitled him ' IN ANY OF HIS
' MAJESTY'S COURTS OF RECORD,' viz.---
' *to recover his treble cofts, befides damages,*
' *which damages fo to be given,* (fays the act)
' *fhall not be lefs than* FIVE HUNDRED POUNDS,'
that is *five hundred pounds* from *each* offen-
dor,—frm *every individual* concerned (and
thefe feem, in the prefent cafe, to have been
more than 4 or 5) that had either been ' *ad-
vifing, aiding,* or ' *affifting,*' in fo flagrant a
breach of the peace ; and they would likewife have been fubject to all the ' *pains, penalties, forfeitures, loffes* or *diffabilities* ordained
in THE STATUTE *of* PROVISION *and* PRÆ-
MUNIRE ! See my ' Reprefentation of the
' injuftice, and dangerous tendency of tole-
' rating Slavery in *England*,' printed in
1769, pages 25 to 29.

GRANVILLE SHARP.

APPEN-

APPENDIX,

(No. 10.)

C A S E,

Prerogative Court, May 11th, 1773.
CAY and CRICHTON.

——A. B. deceafed, *in* 1769, among other effects, left behind him a *negroe fervant.* CRICHTON, the executor, was called upon by CAY, to give in an *inventory* of the deceafed's *goods and chattels,* which he accordingly did, but omitted the *negroe.*

This omiffion was made a ground of exception to the inventory, as being, therefore, not *perfect.*

UPON argument, it was faid by the council on behalf of *Crichton,* that by a very late cafe in the King's Bench, of *Knowles*
and

(a) and *Somerfet*, negroes were declared *to be free in England*, and confequently, they could not be the fubjects of *property*, or be confidered as any part of a perfonal eftate. ⟨*⟩

It was anfwered, that the cafe abovementioned was determined only in 1772; that A. B. died in 1769, at which time negroes were in fome refpects, confidered as property, and therefore that he ought to have been included in the account,

The judge (Dr. *Hay*,) faid that this court had no right to try any queftion relating to freedom and flavery; but as *Negroes* had been *declared free* by the court which had the proper jurifdiction, that determination referred to them, as well at the preceeding time, as at the prefent, and therefore directed, that article, in which the *negroe* was mentioned, to be ftruck out of the *exceptive allegation.*

(a) *Knowles* was the mafter of the fhip who detained *Somerfet*, by order of Mr. *Stewart*, who claimed the latter as his *property.*

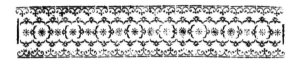

A P P E N D I X,

(No. 11.)

High Court of Admiralty, before Sir Geo.
Hay, *Knt. L.L.D.* June, 29, 1776.

C A S E.

ROGERS, alias *RIGGES* againſt *JONES.*

Dr. *Wynne*	Dr. *Harris*
Dr- *Bever*	Dr. *Calvert*
Proſtor *Torriano.*	Proſtor *Holman.*

' GEORGE ROGERS alias RIGGES,
' a negro about nineteen years of age, had
' been a ſervant to ſeveral gentle en in
' *England,* and in the ſummer of 1766,
' being

' being then out of place, became ac-
' quainted with *John Latter* and *John*
' *Seffins*, who contracted with *Arthur Jones*
' for the sale of him; an assignment
' was accordingly drawn for that- purpose,
' and signed by *John Latter*, by which
' *Rogers* was transferred to Messrs. *Mason*
' and *Jones*, as a slave. for the sum of
' twelve guineas.

' SOME time in August, 1766, after the
' sale above mentioned, *Rogers*, under some
' false pretences, was carried on board the
' ship *Britannia*, then lying at *Deptford*, of
' which Messrs. *Mason* and *Jones* were owners,
' was there detained against his will, and that
' he might not escape, was carried down into
' the sail room, by order of the chief mate,
' and the gratings were put upon him.   In
' this confinement he was kept, till the ship
' set sail, when he was released, and suffer-
' ed to go about upon deck; but, not being
' entered in the ship's books as a mariner,
' nor having any particular office, or wages
' assigned to him, he was set to work about
' the ship's duty in general till he was ap-
' pointed as an assistant to the cook, which
' office he executed sometimes as assistant,
' and sometimes as principal cook, during
' the whole voyage.   The ship first sailed to
' the coast of *Africa*, on the SLAVE TRADE,
                                        and

' and from thence to *Porto Rico*, where he
' was offered to fale, by the captain of
' the *Britannia*, as a prime flave; but
' *Rogers* having found an opportunity
' of relating his ftory to the *Spanifh*
' merchants, they refufed to purchafe
' him; he therefore returned with the
' fhip, in which he ftill acted in his
' former capacity of affiftant cook; and
' upon their arrival in the port of *Lon-*
' *don*, in *May* 1768, when the other ma-
' riners were paid and difcharged, he
' was ftill detained on board againft his
' will.

  ' HERE he continued for fome time, till
' he contrived to give the officers the flip,
' and by the affiftance and advice of fome
' friends, went to *Doctors Commons*, and ap-
' plied to Mr. *Faulckner*, a proctor, to put
' him in a way of recovering his wages, or
' fome other recompence for his labour.
' Mr. *Faulckner* accordingly wrote to
' *Arthur Jones*, one of the owners, for
' that purpofe; and *Rogers* being ap-
' pointed likewife to meet *Jones* at the
' proctor's office, was waiting at a pub-
' lic houfe, in *Doctors Commons*, till fent
' for; when *Jones*, *Seffins*, and another
' man, came into the houfe, forced *Ro-*

  I   ' *gers*

' *gers* into a coach, conveyed him back,
' and forced him on board another fhip,
' where he was chained to the main-
' maft, till he was releafed by the deputy-
' marfhal of the High Court of Admiralty,
' with the affiftance of Mr. *Shea*, one of his
' old mafters, and fome other friends, who
' had obtained a warrant to take him out of
' his confinement.

' Several reafons prevented his ap-
' plying for redrefs of thefe injuries,
' till the beginning of the year 1774,
' when Mr. *Torriano* was employed to
' commence an action againft *Arthur*
' *Jones*, as one of the owners, for the
' purpofe of recovering the ufual wages,
' or fome other recompence in lieu there-
' of.

' After the ufual proceedings, the
' caufe was brought for hearing on June,
' 29, 1776; when the facts being all
' clearly proved as above ftated, the prin-
' cipal queftion was,——*How far the plea*
' *of SLAVERY, fet up by the defendant,*
' *could be admitted in bar of the demand of*
' *wages ?*

' It was infifted on by the counfel on be-
' half of *Rogers*, that the kind of flavery,
' here fpoken of, never had any exiftence
' under the laws of *England*; and in fupport
' of that, referred to the well known Cafe
                                          of

' of *Knowles* and *Somerſet*, before lord,
' *Mansfield* ; and likewiſe to a late one
' in the PREROGATIVE COURT, of *Cay* and
' *Crichton.*

' THE counſel for the defendant argu-
' ed, that, till the caſe of *Somerſet*, the
' law of *England* admitted ſlavery; and
' in ſupport of this, they quoted the au-
' thority of Lord Chief Juſtice *Hale*; and,
' in particular, the opinions of the Lords
' *Talbot* and *Hardwick.*'

THE Decree of the Court thereupon was,
in ſubſtance, as follows.

' *THERE are two principal points in*
' *this cauſe* ; (ſaid the Judge)
' 1ſt. *Whether ſuch a ſervice is proved (as*
' *ſtated in the ſummary Petition) as to enti-*
' *tle the plaintiff to the wages demanded? and*
' 2dly. *Whether the plea of ſlavery ſhall be*
' *a ſufficient bar to the claim?*

' *With regard to the* FIRST, *it appears by*
' *the fulleſt evidence, that the plaintiff had ſerv-*
' *ed on board the ſhip, either in the capacity*
' *of aſſiſtant to the cook, or as cook himſelf,*
' *during the greateſt part of the voyage, and*
' *conſequently was entitled to ſome recompence*
' *for his ſervices* ; *but not being entered as a*
' *mariner in the ſhip's books, nor having any*
'   ' *ſtipulated*

' *stipulated wages affigned him; it being proba-*
' *ble that the owners meant to fell him again in*
' *the West Indies, he cannot be allowed any fpe-*
' *cific fum under the name of* WAGES; *but as*
' *he certainly performed the duty to which he*
' *was affigned, without any objection to his be-*
' *haviour in it, the maritime law clearly gives*
' *him a* QUANTUM MERUIT. *The cook's*
' *wages appear to have been* £1. 5s. 6d. *per*
' *Month, which is more than* Rogers, *moft*
' *probably, could fairly deferve. But upon in-*
' *fpection of the mariners contract, it appears*
' *that there were feveral negroe boys in the*
' *fame fhip, in the quality of apprentices, who*
' *were allowed from* 10s. *to* 17s. *and* 6d. *per*
' *month ;'* he fignified his opinion therefore,
that Rogers *might fairly deferve* 15s. *per
month,* which he accordingly decreed him,
from the time of his being firft carried on
board

' *With regard to the* SECOND *point, it was*
' *urged* (faid the judge) *that the plaintiff was*
' *a* SLAVE, *and confequently was not entitled to*
' *any reward for his fervice at all*

' *The practice of buying and felling flaves*
' *(the learned judge remarked) was cer-*
' *tainly very common in* England, *before*
' *the cafe of* SOMERSET, *in the Court of*
' *King's Bench,* 1772, *but however it might*
' *have been the law of the Royal Ex-*
' *change*

' change,' he hoped, ' it never was the law of
' England.

' The OPINIONS of lord Hardwicke, and
' lord Talbot, when Attorney and Solicitor
' general, have been quoted in support of this
' practice, and have formerly given too much
' countenance to it, though they seemed origi-
' nally to have been only applied to the diffe-
' rence created by baptism.'

' But by a late determination of one of the
' ablest judges that ever presided in this king-
' dom, these opinions have been held to be mif-
' taken and unsound; and there can be no fur-
' ther doubt, that the claim of SLAVERY is not
' maintainable by the laws of England.

' The law therefore was the same before the
' time of the above opinions, as since; and, con-
' sequently, refers to all sales whatsoever of
' this nature; which are every ore illegal: and
' therefore the pretended sale in the present
' case, in 1766, was an absolute nullity; and
' when the allegation, stating the sale, was
' admitted on behalf of the owners, had Rogers
' appeared, under protest, upon this point of
' law, it would have been received in bar of
' the plea!

' The owners seem to have acted upon a
' mistaken notion of their right; but as the
' claim of slavery is clearly against the law of
' this country, and as it appeared that Rogers
                                        ' had

' *had always aEted in fome ufeful capacity dur-*
' *ing the whole time of his having been on*
' *board,*' the judge faid, he thought *him*
' *entitled to a* QUANTUM MERUIT *for his*
' *fervice,*'——which he accordingly fixed as
above; and condemned the owners in cofts;
which were immediately taxed to the amount
of £81. 11s. 0d.

APPEN-

A P P E N D I X,

(No. 12.)

From the General Evening Poft, No.
6033. *June* 13th, 1772.

To the Editor of the General Evening Poft.

S I R,

AS the great caufe depending between
Mr. *Stuart*, and *Somerfet*, the negro,
is at prefent one of the principal topics of
general converfation, by inferting the following you will afford a feafonable and rational entertainment to your readers. I am
your's, &c.

Extract of a letter from a perfon in Maryland, *to his friend in* Philadelphia.

' I am fo happy as to think as you do,
' with regard to trading in man, or keep-
' ing

' ing him a flave. The cuftom is wicked
' and iniquitous, neither confiftent with
' reafon, or the laws of God or man.
' Poor unhappy flaves, particularly thofe
' forced from their places of nativity, are
' moft certainly deplorable objects of com-
' miferation. I never bought more than
' two during twenty years refidence here.
' One proved to be the fon of an African
' Prince; he was a moft comely youth: hav-
' ing obferved his uncommon good parts,
' I fent him to fchool, and ufed him like
' a free man during his ftay with me. The
' directors of the African Company having
' enquired, and offered a reward for him,
' I by a public act prefented the poor crea-
' ture with his freedom, gave him an order
' for the reward aforefaid, and fent him to
' London; from whence the following year
' he remitted me the fame fum he coft me,
' and fundry rich goods to the amount of
' three hundred pounds and upwards, and
' therewith a letter in his own native lan-
' guage, tranflated by Dr. Defaguillier, of
' Cambridge.

' The next I purchafed was an unhap-
' py lad, kidnapped from his free pa-
' rents at the taking of Guadaloupe.
' During his ftay with me he decayed or
' pined fo much, and expreffed fo fenfible
' a forrow of cruel feparation from his
                                        ' aged

' aged parents, relations, and countrymen,
' that actuated by the unerring good provi-
' dence which directs us in all our good deeds,
' I likewife fet this poor creature free, and
' fent him to his native place. Providence
' again would not excufe my being further
' rewarded, for performing this my duty
' as a Chriftian. The truly honeft father,
' from the produce of his plantations, has
' made me prefents to the amount of fifty
' pounds fterling, with direction to draw
' upon him for the full coft of the poor
' youth, which I do never intend, being
' more than paid by prefents.

' I write this to convince you that the in-
' habitants of Africa are not fuch fenfelefs
' brutifh creatures as thoughtlefs authors
' reprefent them to be: they undoubtedly
' are capable of receiving inftruction, and
' far out-do Chriftians in many commend-
' able virtues. Poor creatures! their great-
' eft unhappinefs is being acquainted with
' *Chriftians.* ‡

‡ The worthy and benevolent writer muft mean
fuch *Chriftians* only as thofe, who carry out with them
nothing of that moft amiable profeffion of religion
but *the name*, to the ' *fhip wrack*,' of their own fouls,
and to the difgrace of their native country, if that alfo
is called *Chriftian !*

m　　　　　The

' The following is a letter from the
' Negro Prince, fome time after he
' arrived at *London*, to his mafter
' in *Maryland*. Tranflated by Dr.
' *Defaguillier*, of *Cambridge*, 1743.

From the great city, 3d moon after my releafe.

' O my kind merciful mafter, my good
' white brother, too good, a very good fon of
' a good woman, and of a very good old
' man, created good old people by the GREAT
' SPIRIT, who made my country, thy poor
' (I fhould fay heretofore poor) moft grate-
' ful black prifoner, now rendered rich by
' thy goodnefs and mercy, is now moft
' dead, moft drunk, moft mad with joy!
' Why is he fo? becaufe he is going to his
' good warm country, to his good old mo-
' ther, to his good old father, to his little
' fifter and his brother. In my good warm
' country all things are good, except the
' white people who live there, and come in
' flying-houfes to take away poor black prifo-
' ners from their mothers their fathers, their
' fifters and brothers, to kill them with hun-
' ger and filth, in the cellars of their flying-
' houfes, wherein if they do not die faft
                                    ' enough,

' enough, and poor prifoners talk for bread
' and water, and want to feel the wind,
' and to fee THE GREAT SPIRIT, to com-
' plain to him, to tell him all, or to fee the
' trees of his good warm country once
' more for the laft time, the King of the
' white people [*probably the negro meant*
' *the captain*] orders the officer called Jack,
' to kill many of the black prifoners, with
' whips, with ropes, knives, axes and falt.
' The governor of thy flying-houfe has
' been to fhew that which is to carry me and
' him to my good warm country; I am
' glad, very glad indeed! He goes there
' with wine. Should he be fick, (and white
' people feldom efcape being fo there,) be-
' caufe of thee my kind merciful mafter,
' and good white brother, and becaufe he
' has been good to me, and is a very good
' white man too, I will nurfe him myfelf,
' my mother, my father, my little fifter,
' and my brother, fhall be his brother, his
' mother, his father, and his fifter too;
' he fhall have one large heap of ele-
' phants teeth and gold, for thee my kind
' merciful mafter, and kind brother, and
' one for himfelf alfo (but fmaller.) He at
' prefent is my father, I eat at his houfe,
' and lie there too upon the bed thou pre-
' fented me with. His woman is my mo-
                                      ' ther,

‘ ther, and kindly nurfes me, being very
‘ fick of the fea and fire made of black
‘ ftones. I have received a great quantity
‘ of gold, befides what thou did prefent
‘ me with by means of thy hand writing,
‘ to the people who are to fend me to my
‘ country, fome part whereof I have given
‘ to the governor of thy fwimming-houfe,
‘ to be fent to thee; had I an houfeful
‘ fhould fend the whole with equal plea-
‘ fure ; however, thou fhalt fee hereafter,
‘ that black people are not beafts, and do
‘ know how to be grateful. “ After thou my
‘ kind merciful mafter and good white bro-
‘ ther left me in thy fwiming houfe, we,
‘ thy white people, and we thy grateful black
‘ prifoners, were by the GREAT SPIRIT, who
‘ was angry with us, fent by the wind into
‘ an immenfe great river, where we had like
‘ to have been drowned, and where we could
‘ fee neither fun nor moon, for fix days and
‘ nights. I was dying during one who e
‘ moon, the governor was my father, and
‘ gave me thofe good things thou prefented
‘ me with on my bed, he lodged me in the
‘ little room thy carpenter built for me.
‘ Thou gave me more cloaths than I could
‘ carry, yet I was very cold ; nothing avail-
‘ ed with poor black prifoner, till at laft hav-
‘ ing THE GREAT SPIRIT to fend me fafe to
‘ thy houfe on fhore, I thought I was carried
‘ there,

' there, [*this appears to have been a dream*]
' where thou my good white brother did ufe
' me with wonted goodnefs, fpake to THE
' GREAT SPIRIT, and TO HIS SON, that I
' might keep fo during the voyage and af-
' terwards, which they have done for thy
' fake ; they will always do me good becaufe
' of thee my good white brother ; therefore
' my kind merciful mafter, do not forget thy
' poor black prifoner. When thou doft fpeak
' to THE GREAT SPIRIT and TO HIS SON, I
' do know he will hear thee, I fhall never
' be fick more, for which I fhall be thank-
' ful.   Pray fpeak for my good old mother,
' my good father,   y little fifter, and my
' brother ; I wifh they may be healthy, to
' many very many moons, as many as the
' hairs on thy head ; I love them all much, yet
' I think not fo much as I do thee, I could die
' in my country for thee, could I do thee any
' kindnefs. Indeed THE GREAT SPIRIT well
' knows I mean no lie, fhall always fpeak to
' him for thy good, believe me my good
' white brother, thy poor black prifoner is
' not a liar.

Dgiagola, *fon of* Dgiagola, *Prince*
of Foat, ‖ *Africa.*

‖ The country, here called FOAT, is probably named (the found being nearly the fame) from PHUT, the
third fon of *Ham* ; concerning whom, and his defcendants

fcendants in the interior part of *Africa*, particular mention is made in Mr. *Bryant*'s letter, on the defcent of the negroes. See Appendix, No. 4. pages 48 to 52 : or perhaps it may mean ' *the very country upon the ri-* ' *ver Gambia on one fide*,' which (as Mr. *Bryant* informs us from *Bluet*) ' *is at this day called* PHUTA.' See p. 50.

I N D E X

O F

Texts referred to in the foregoing Work.

DEUTERONOMY.

II CHRONICLES.

JOB.

PSALMS.

PROVERBS.

JEREMIAH.

EZEKIEL.

AMOS.

INDEX.

INDEX.

A.

Barbadoes,

B.

C.

Chriftianity,

N.

O.

P.

Planters,

F I N I S.